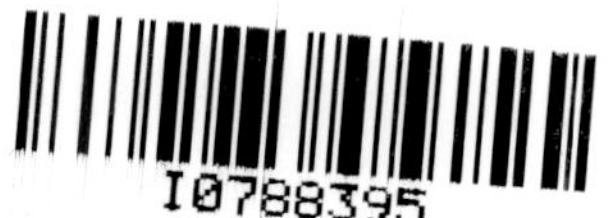
I0788395

DRAGON

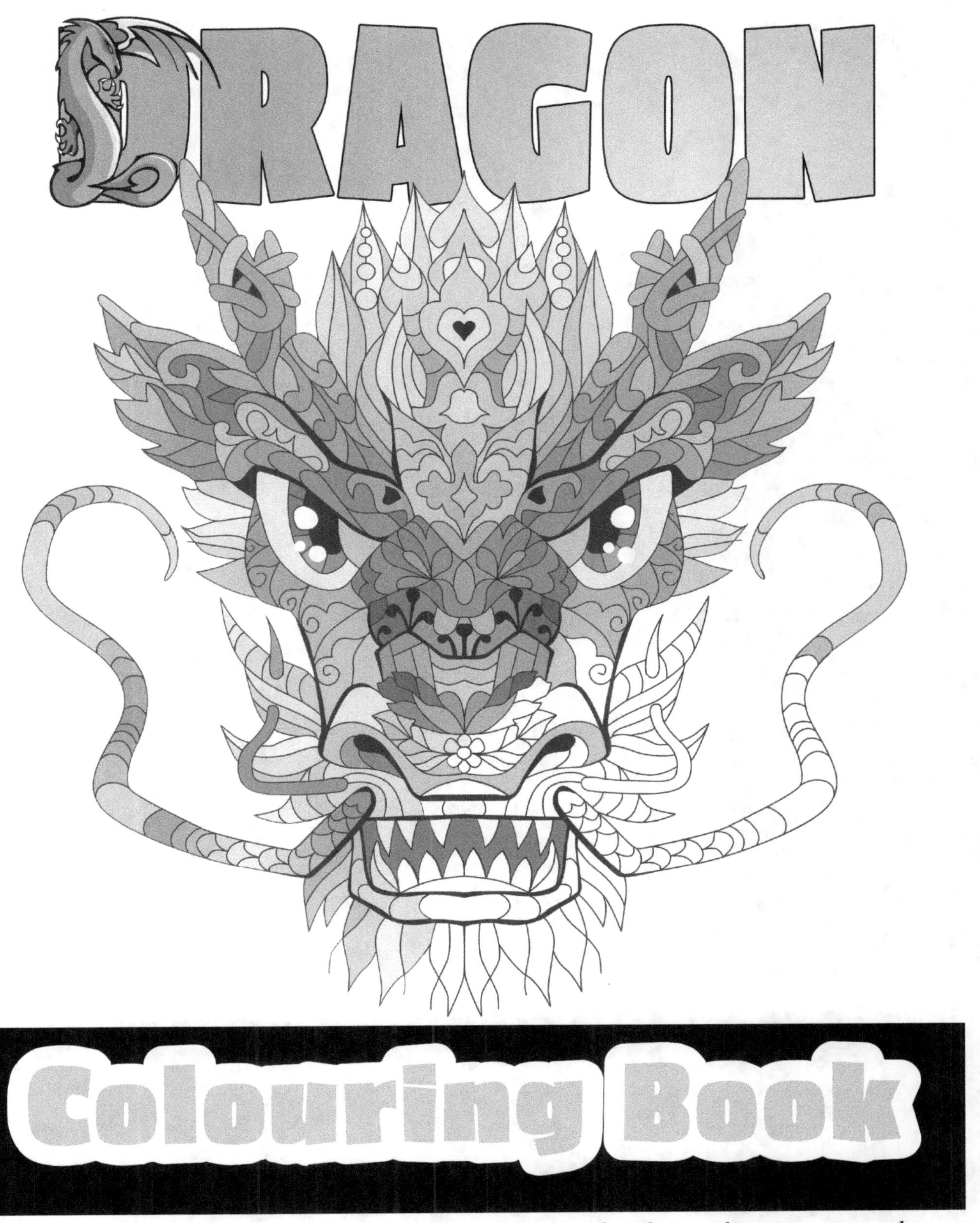

Colouring Book

Copyright © 2020 by Lasting Happiness
ISBN: 978-1-989842-20-1

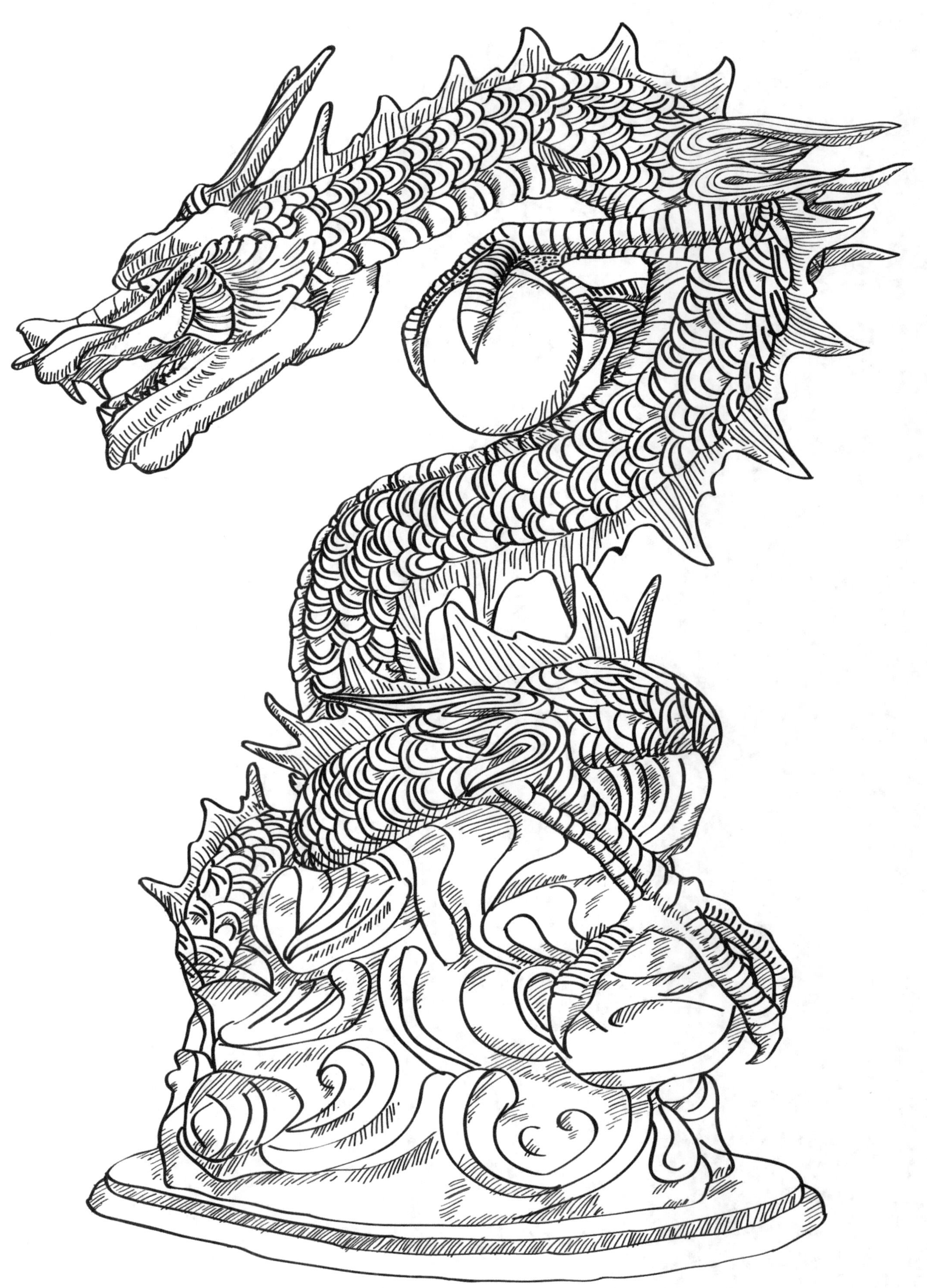

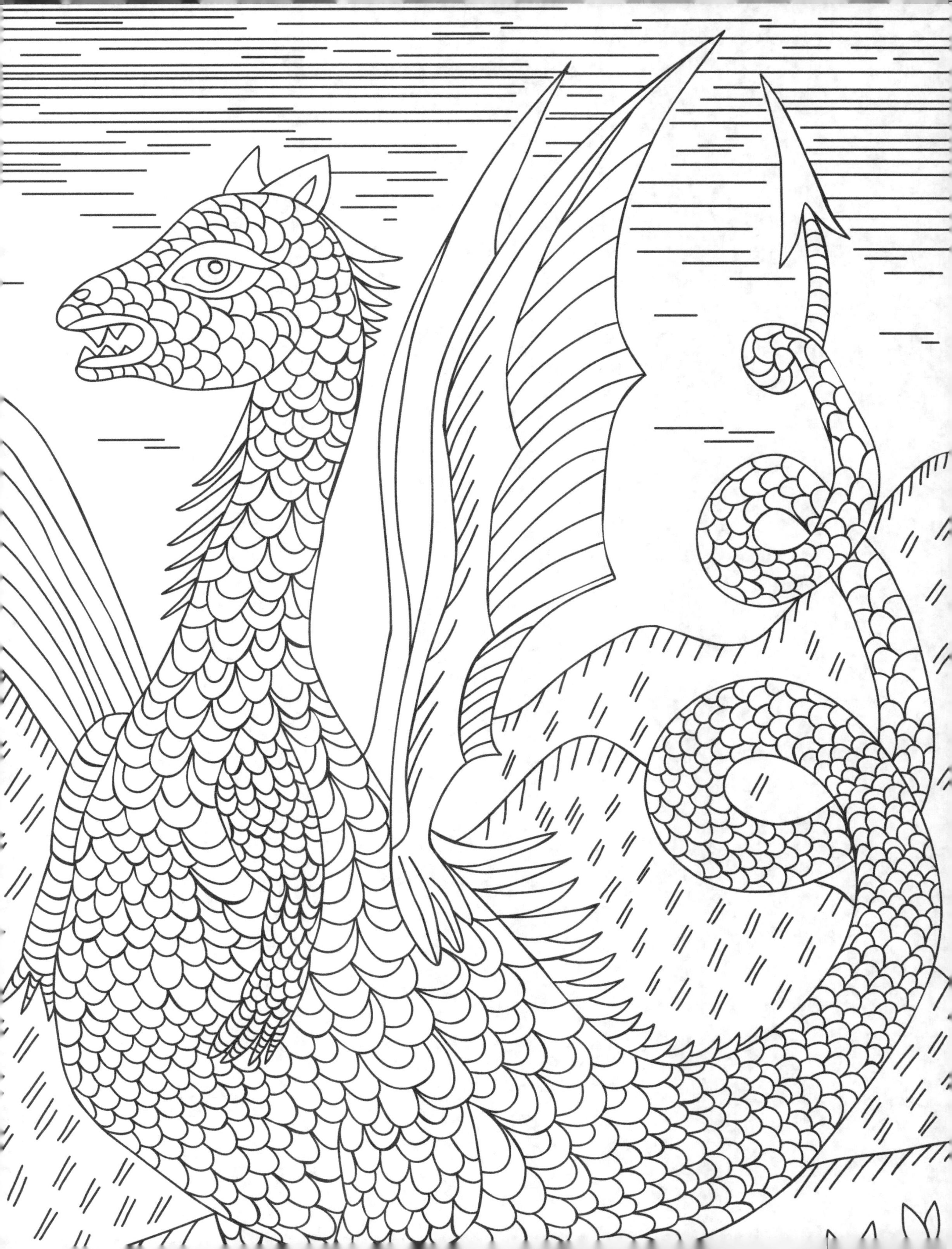

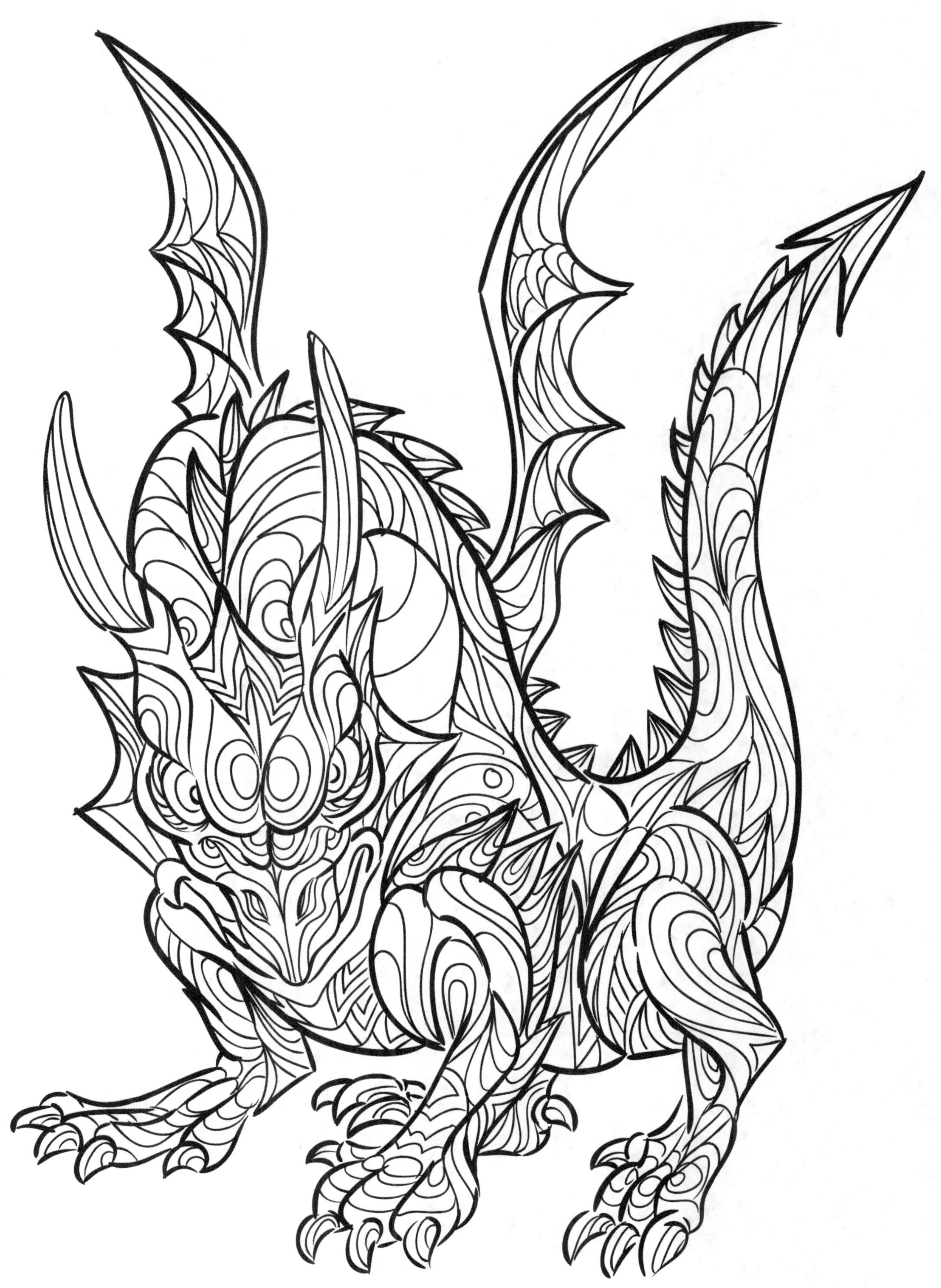

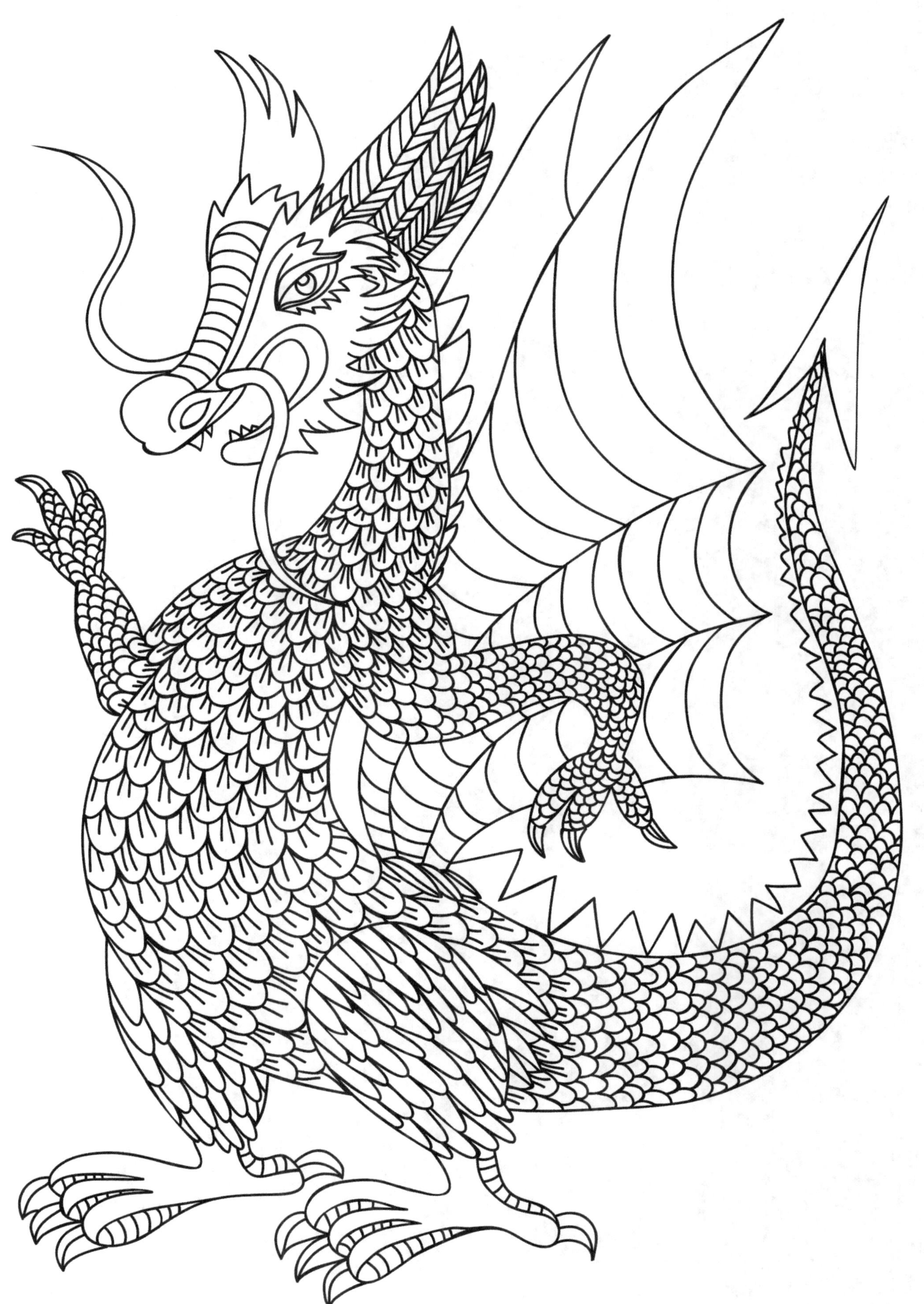

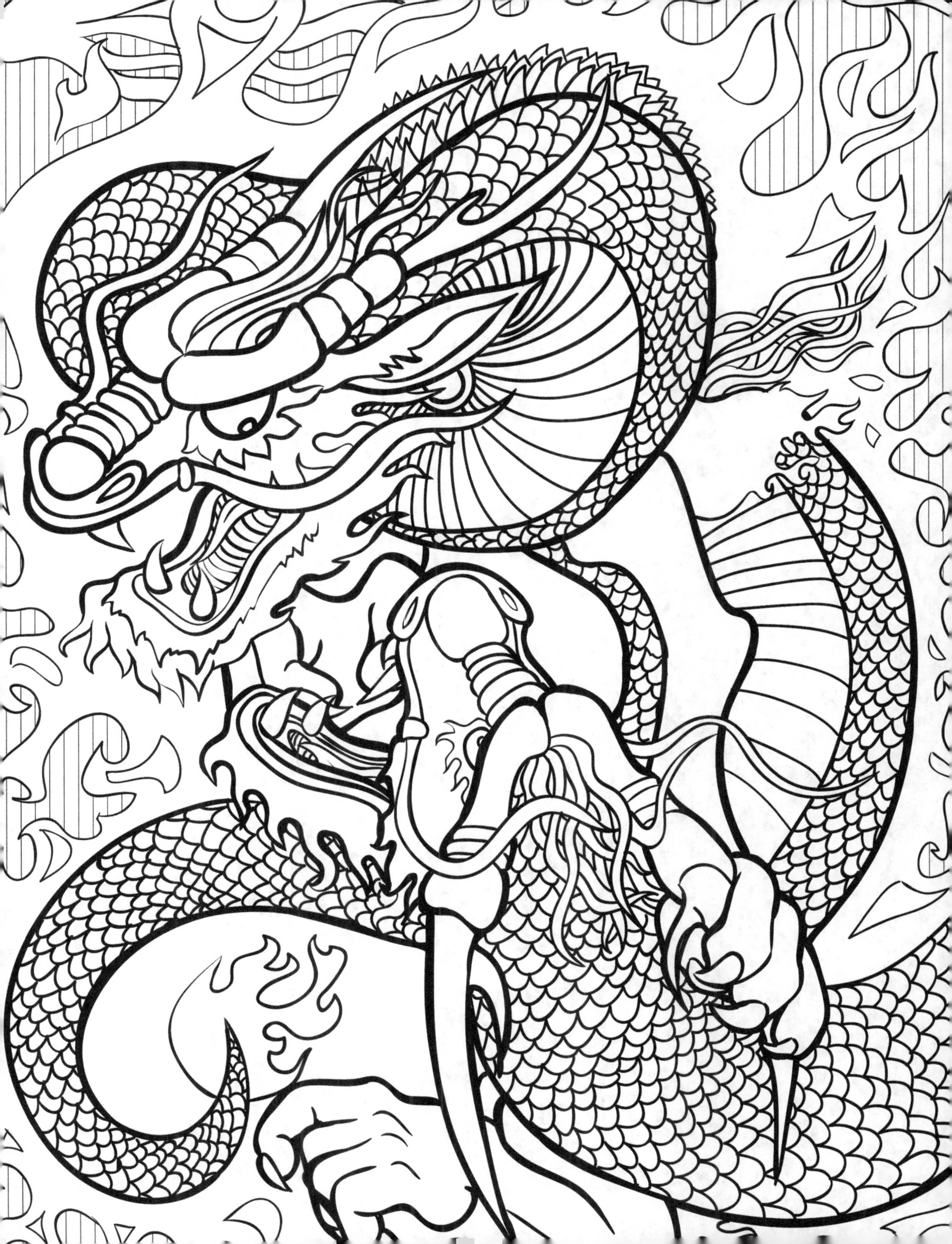

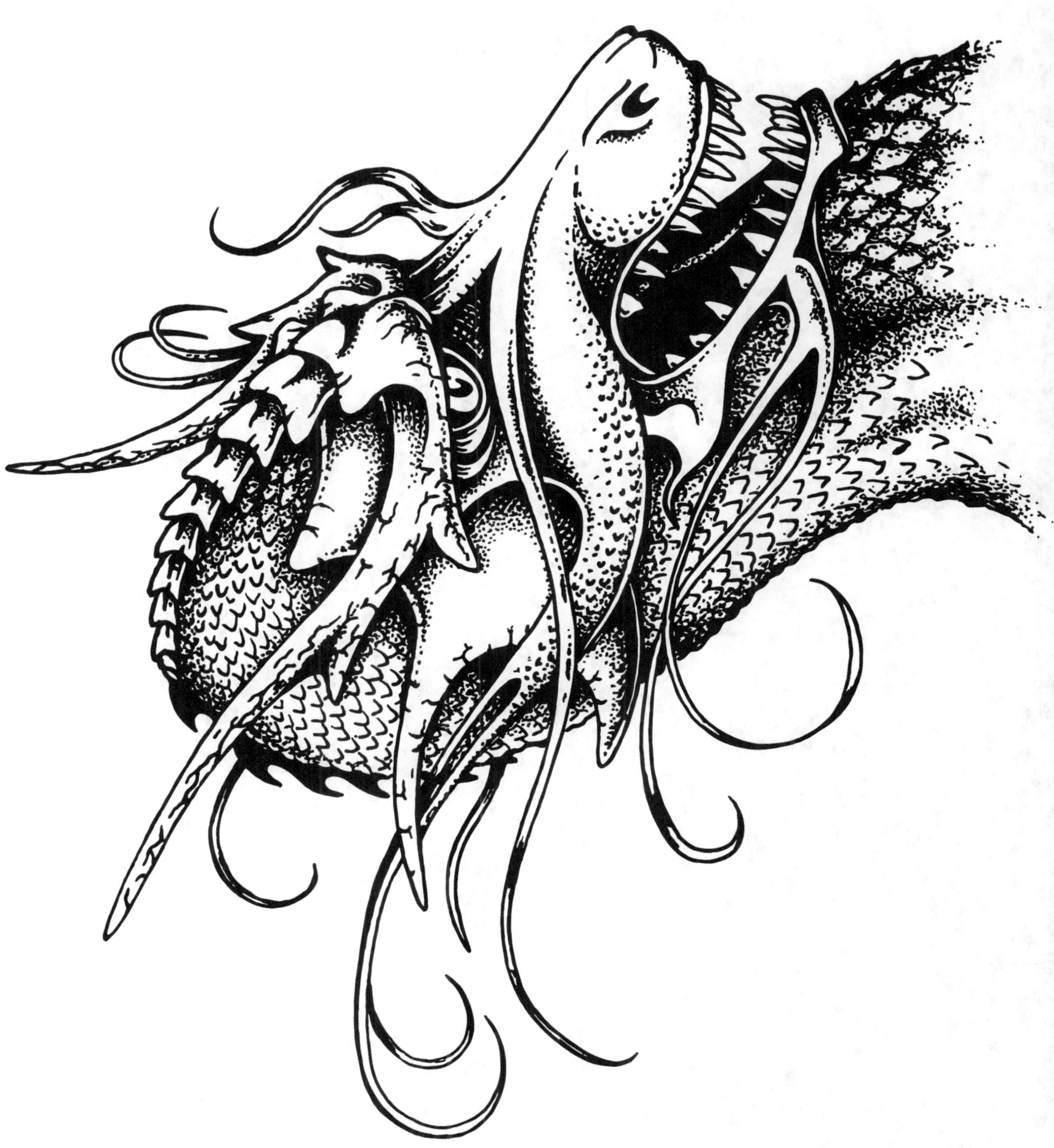

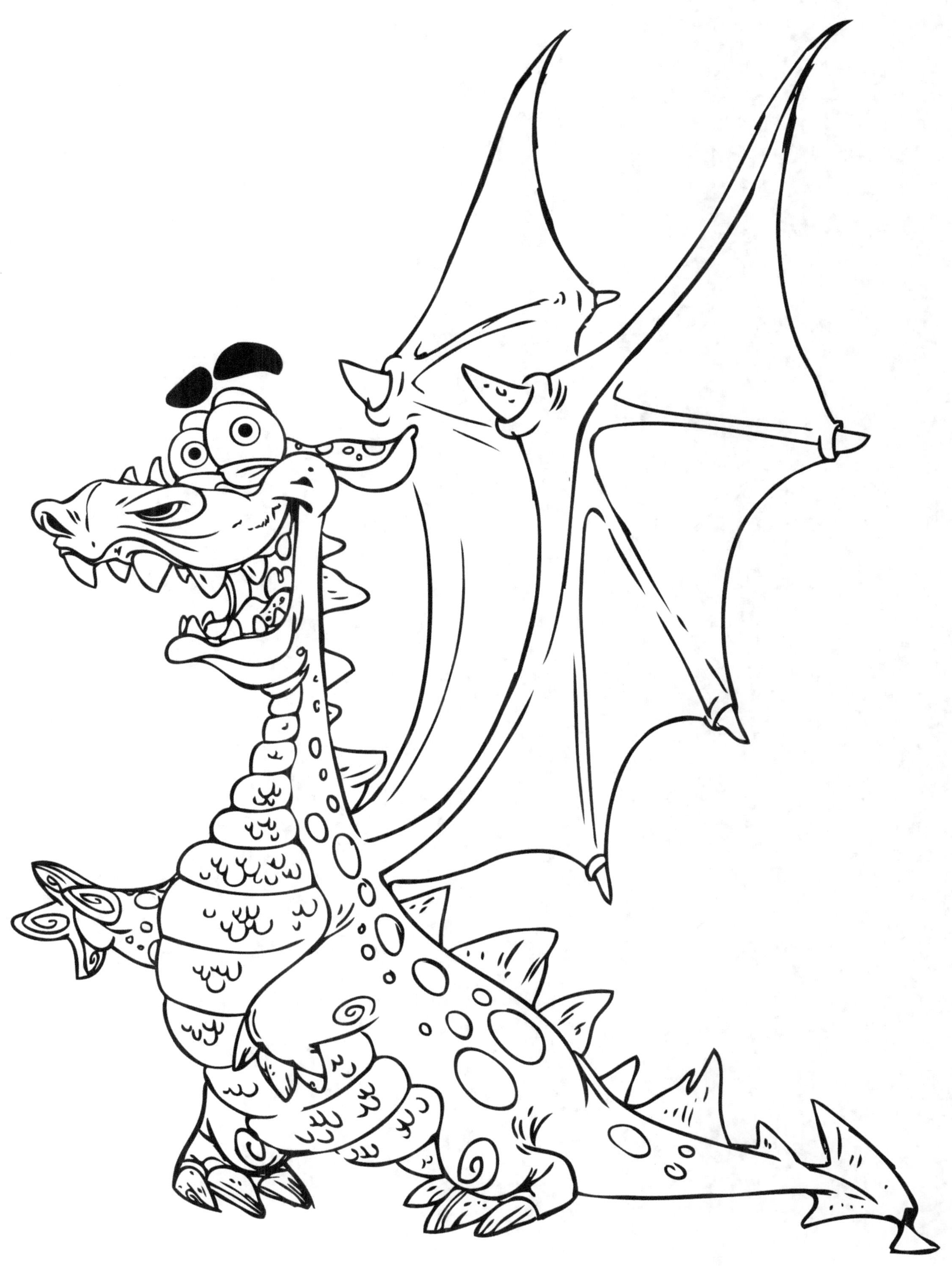

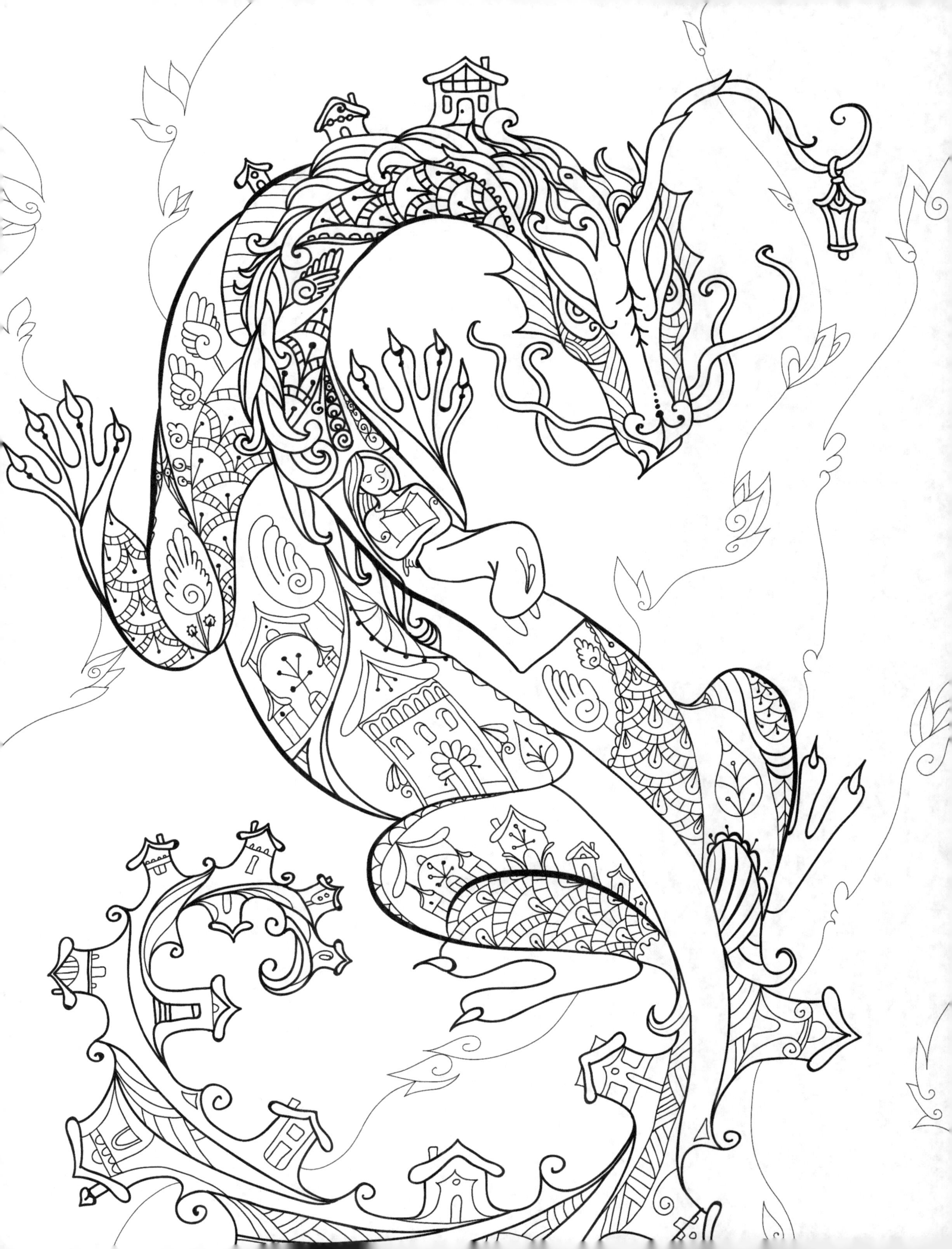

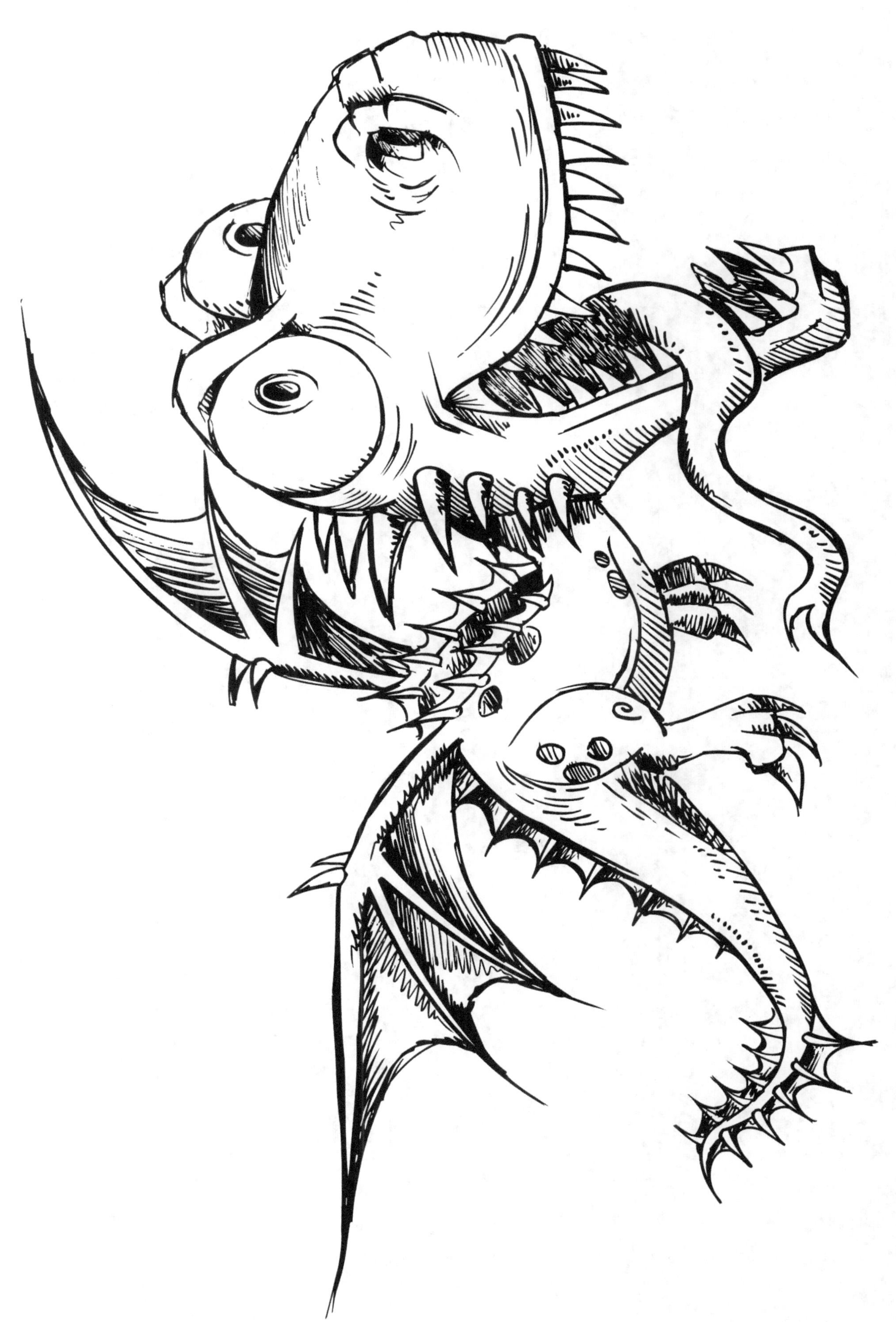

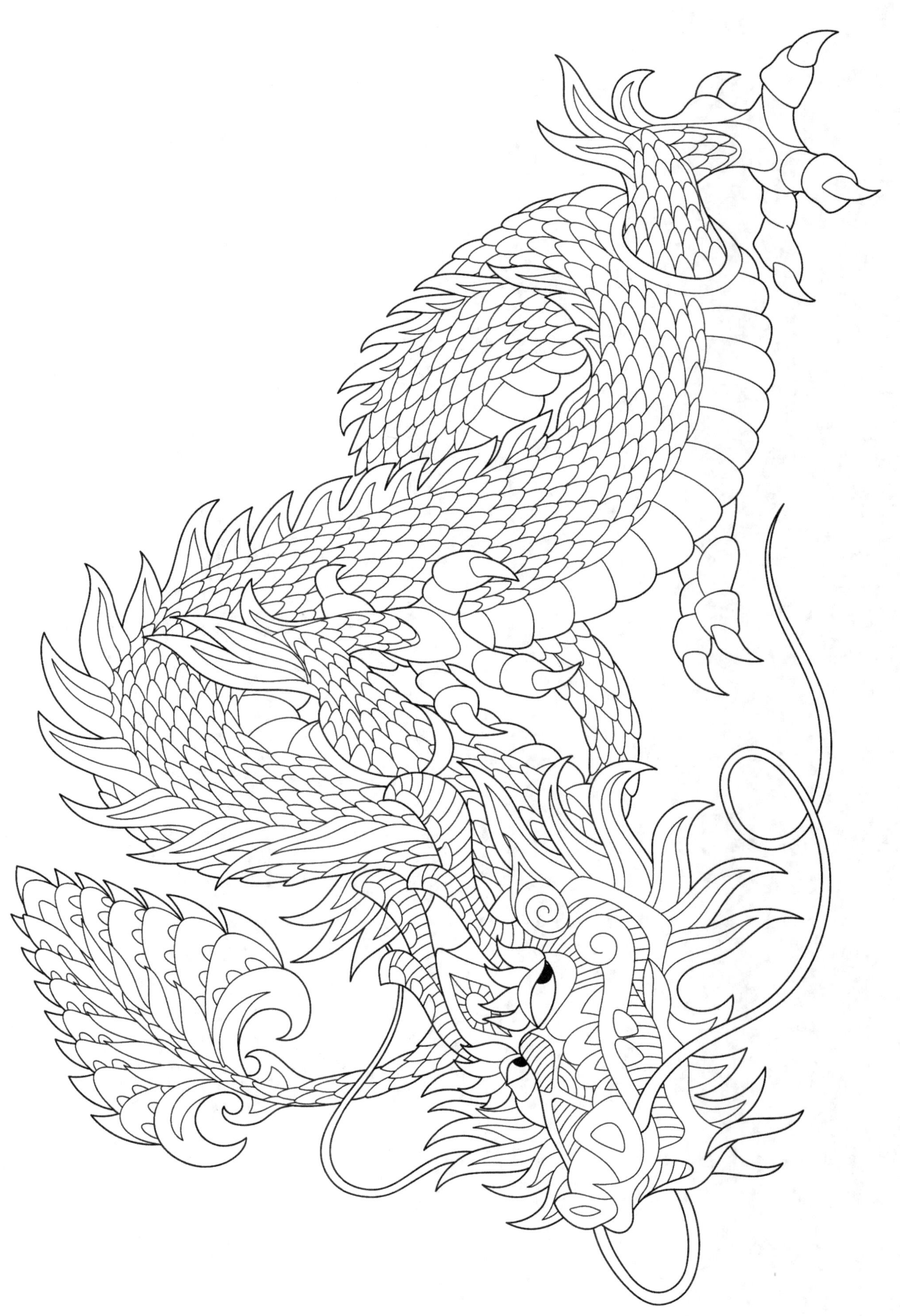

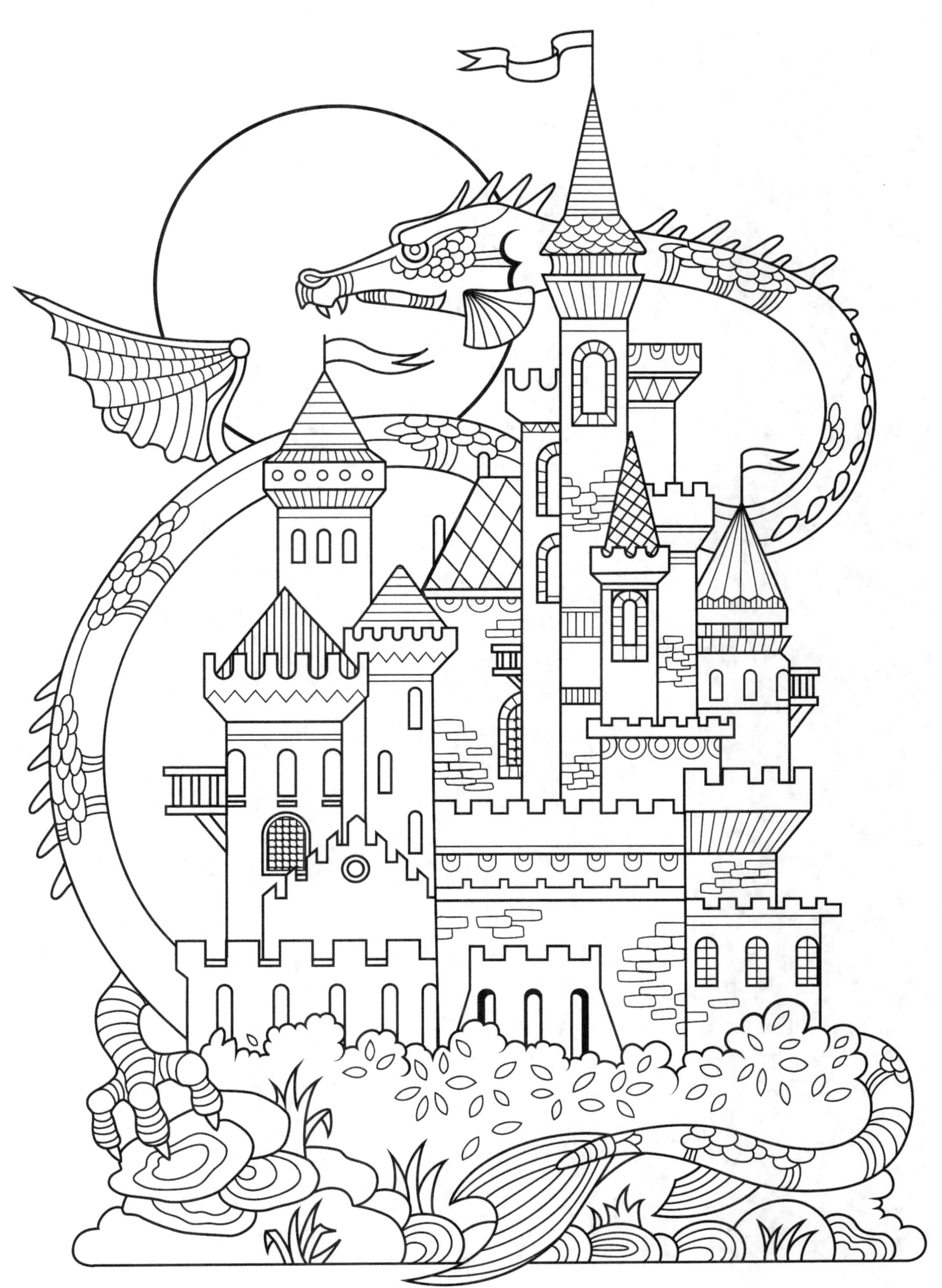

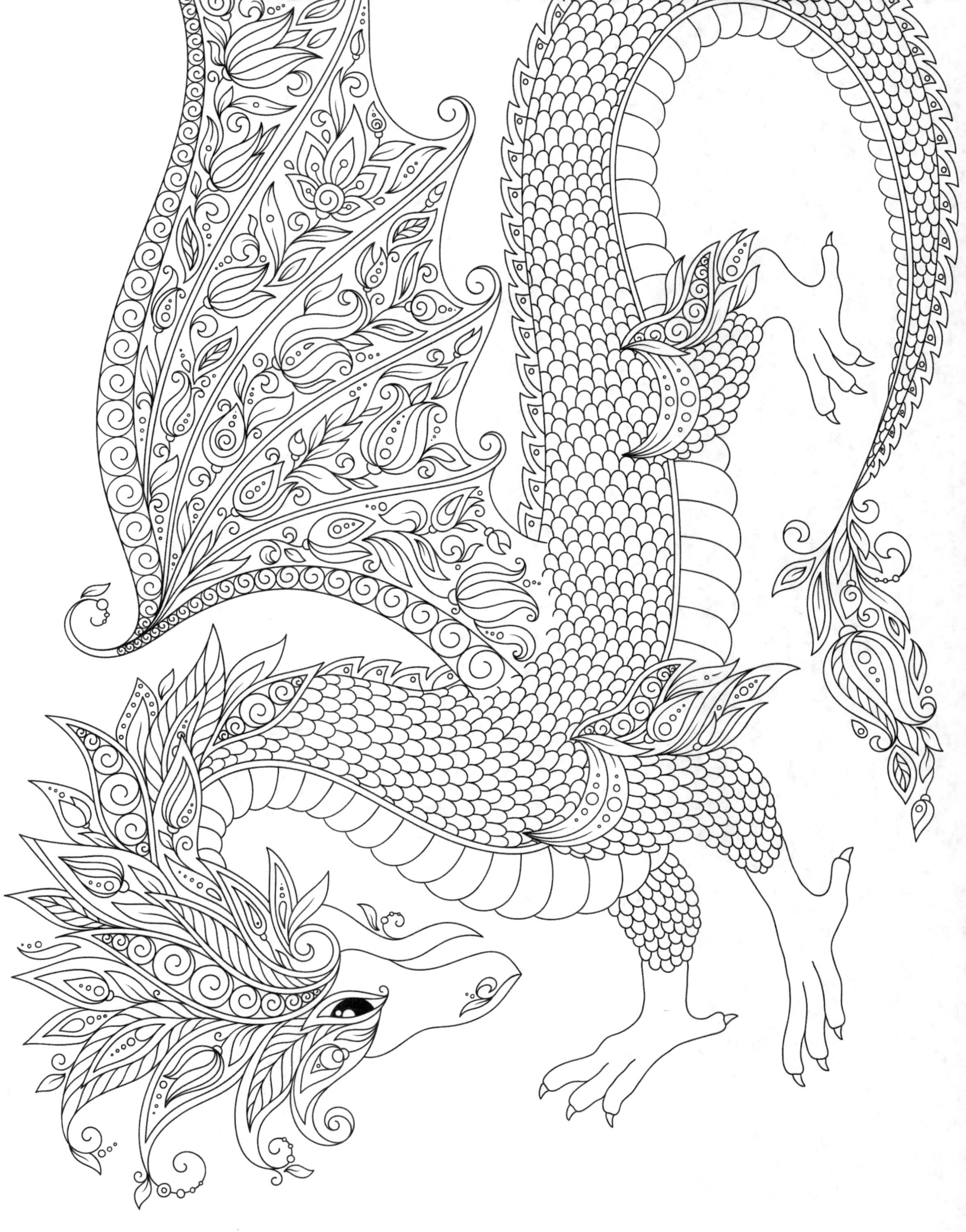

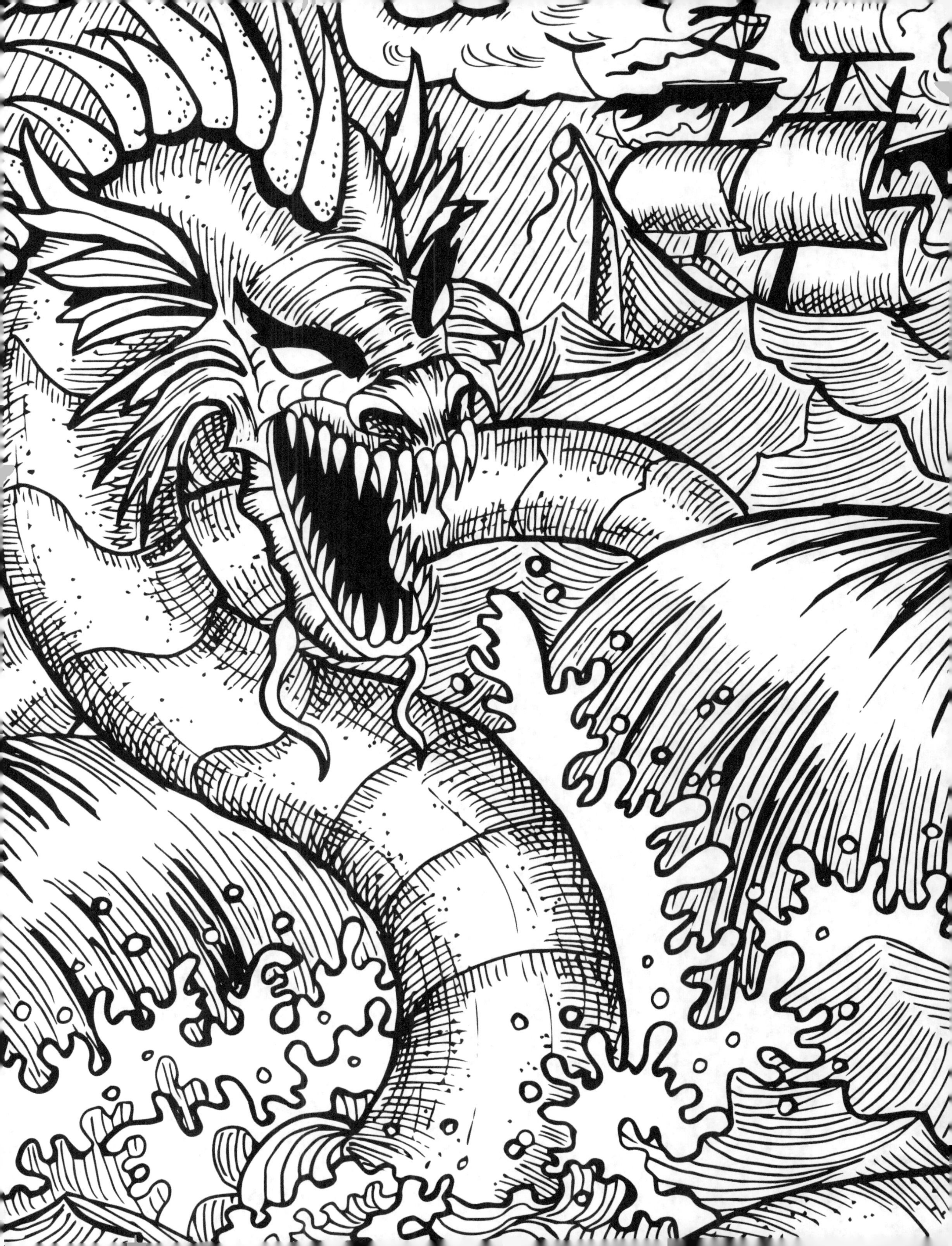

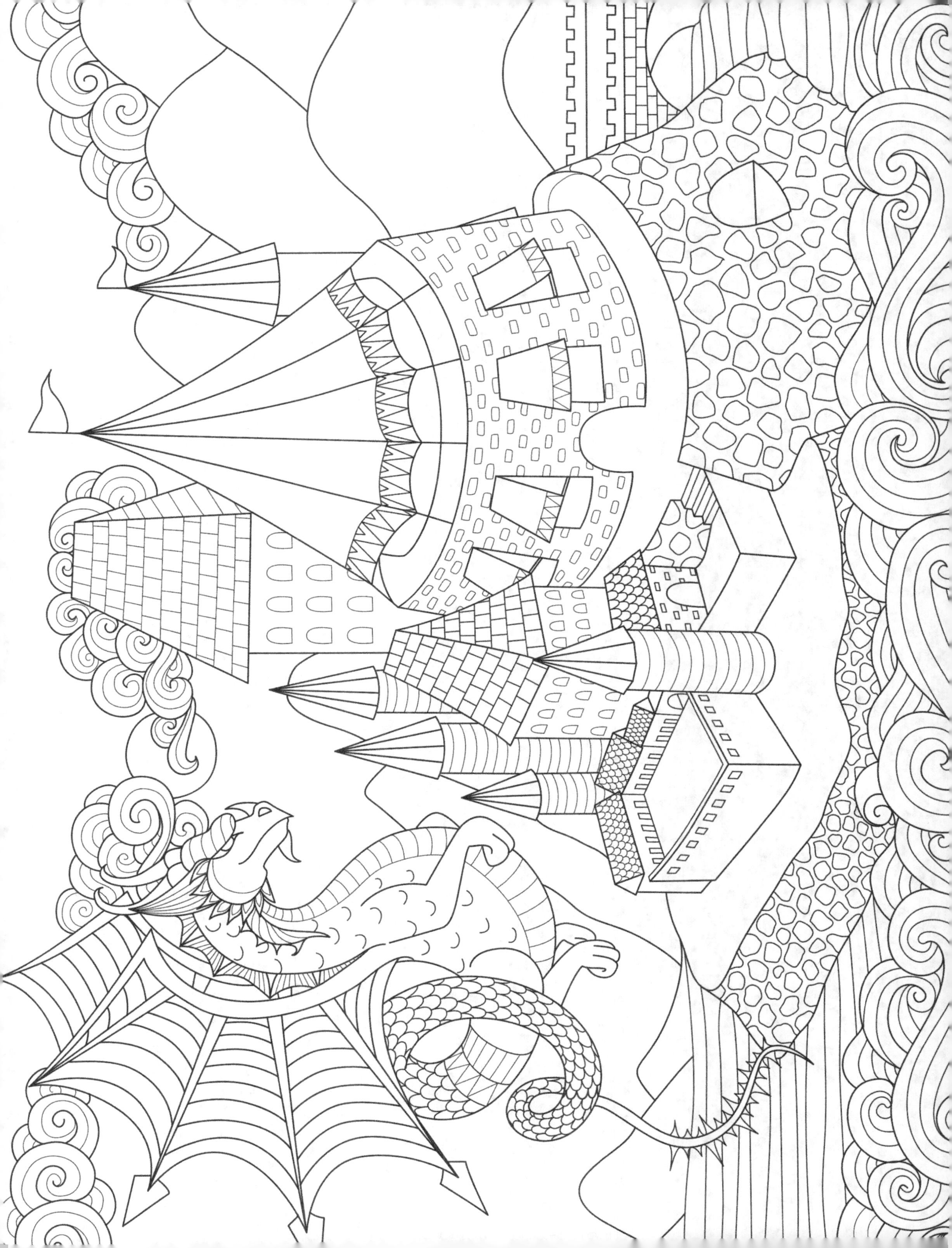

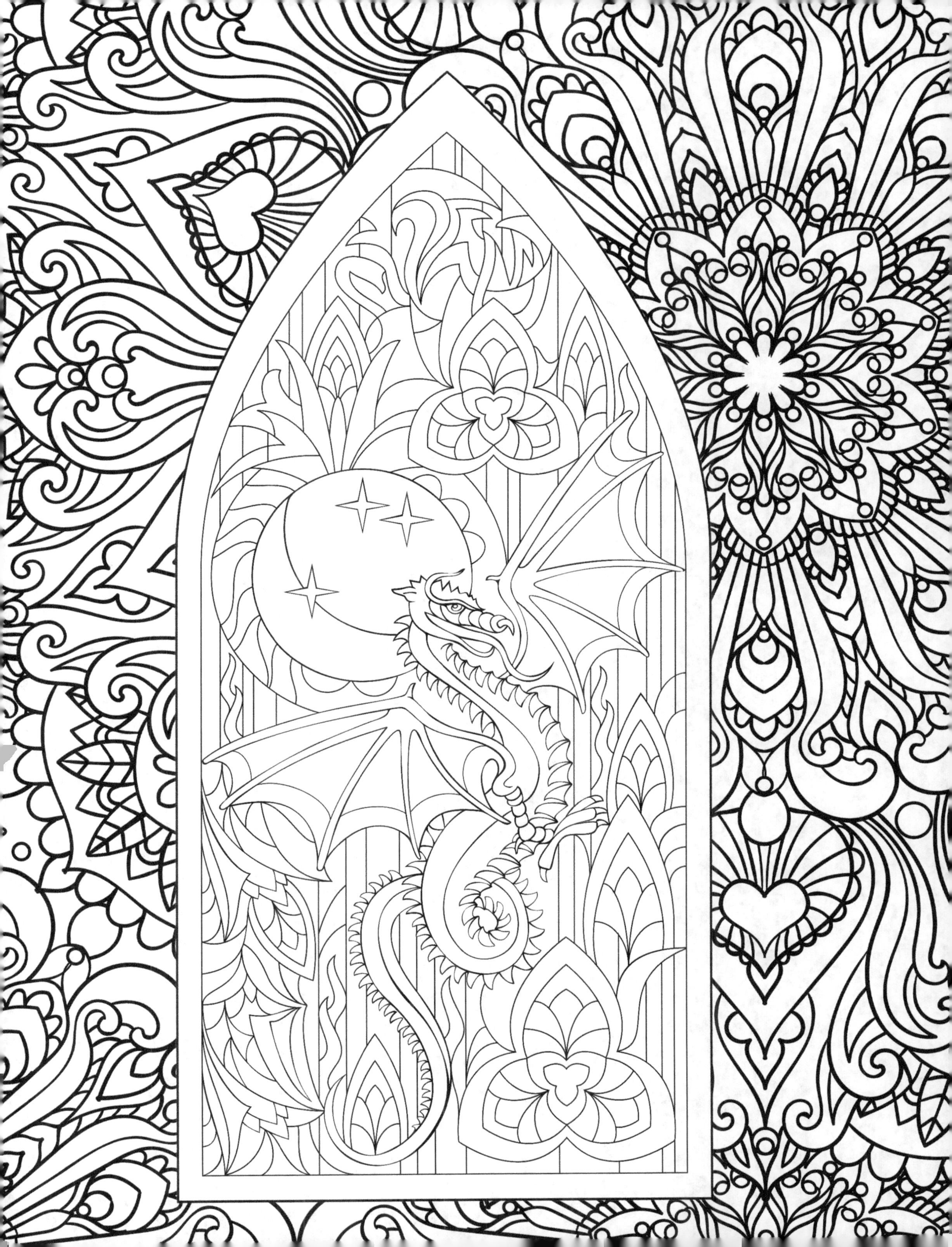

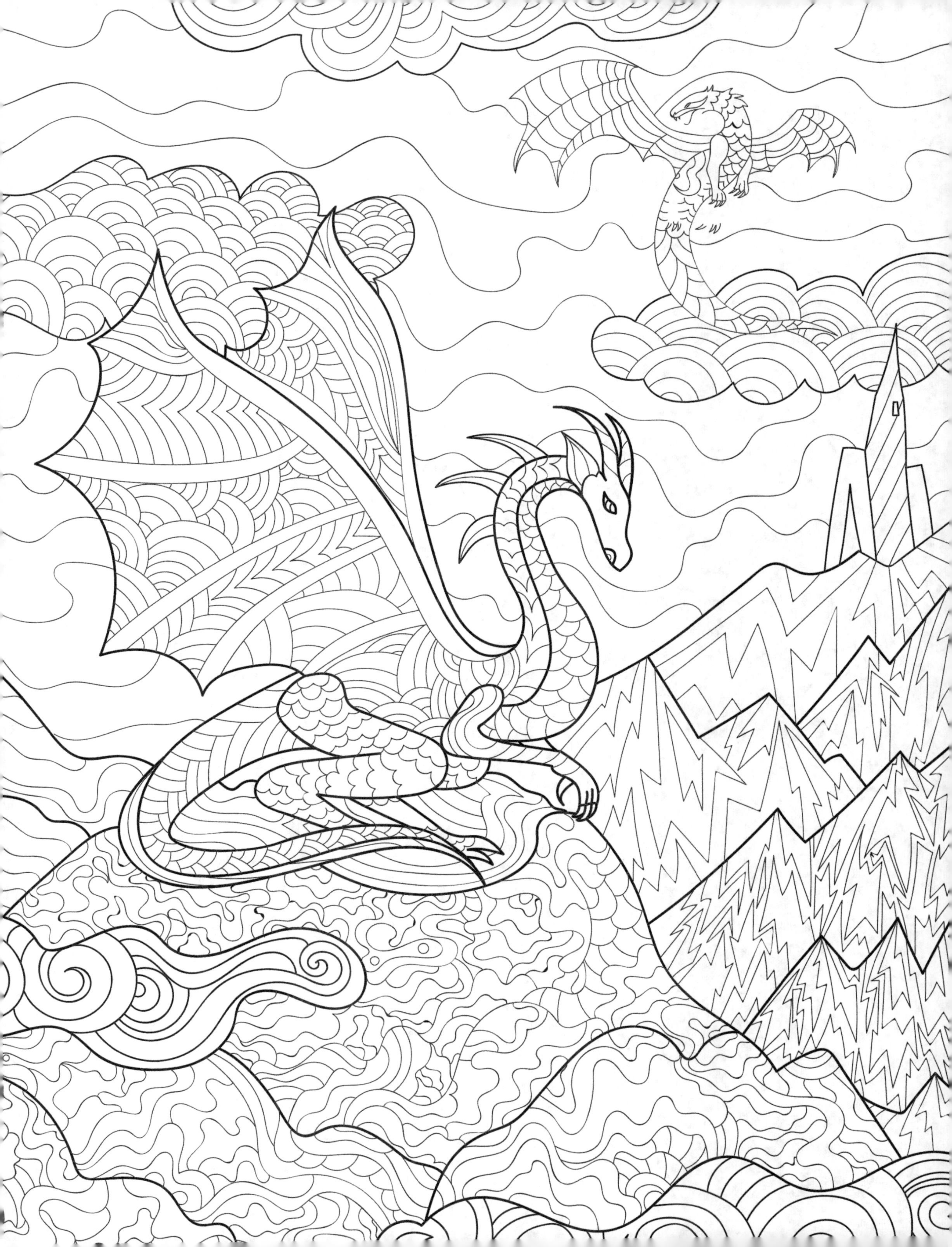

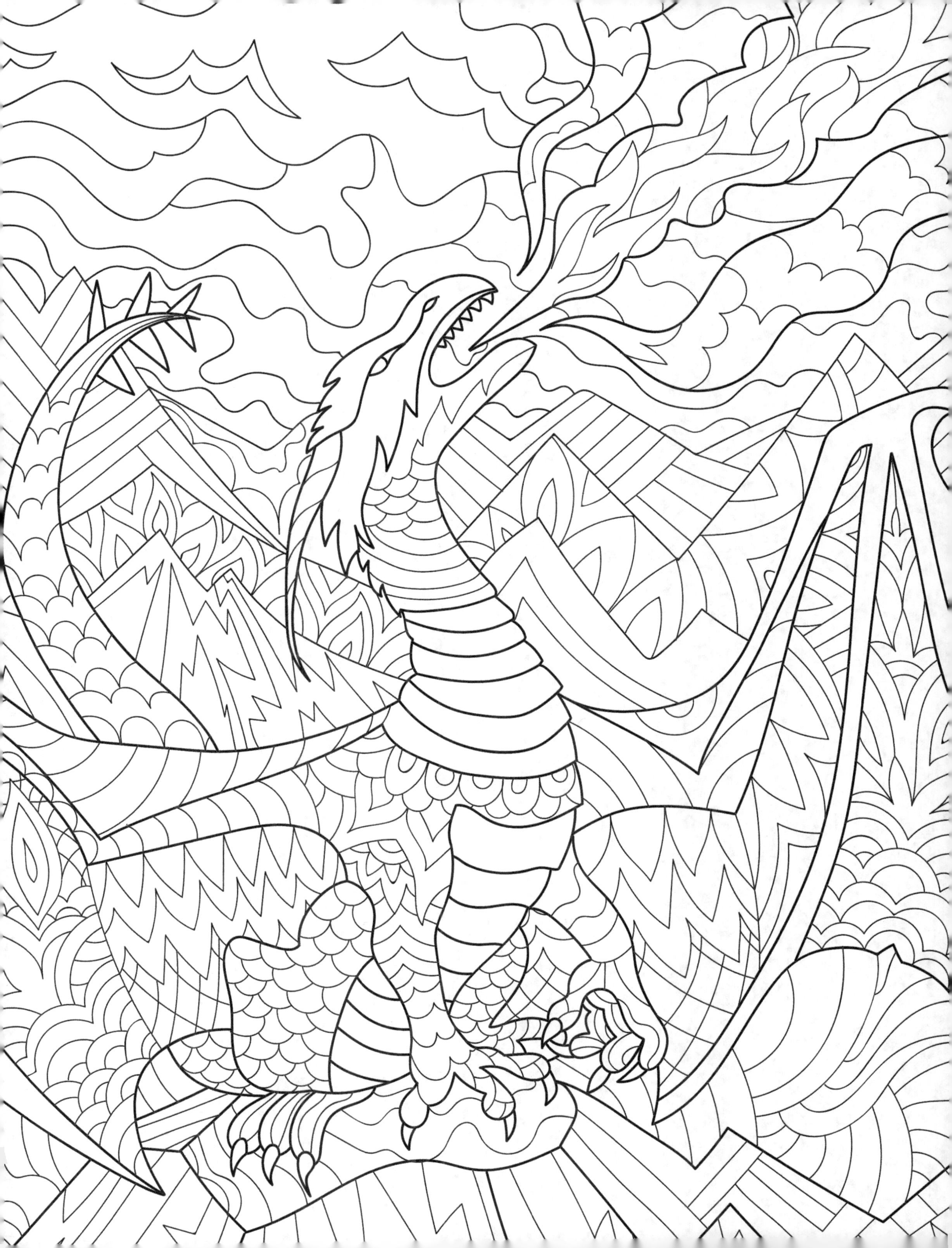

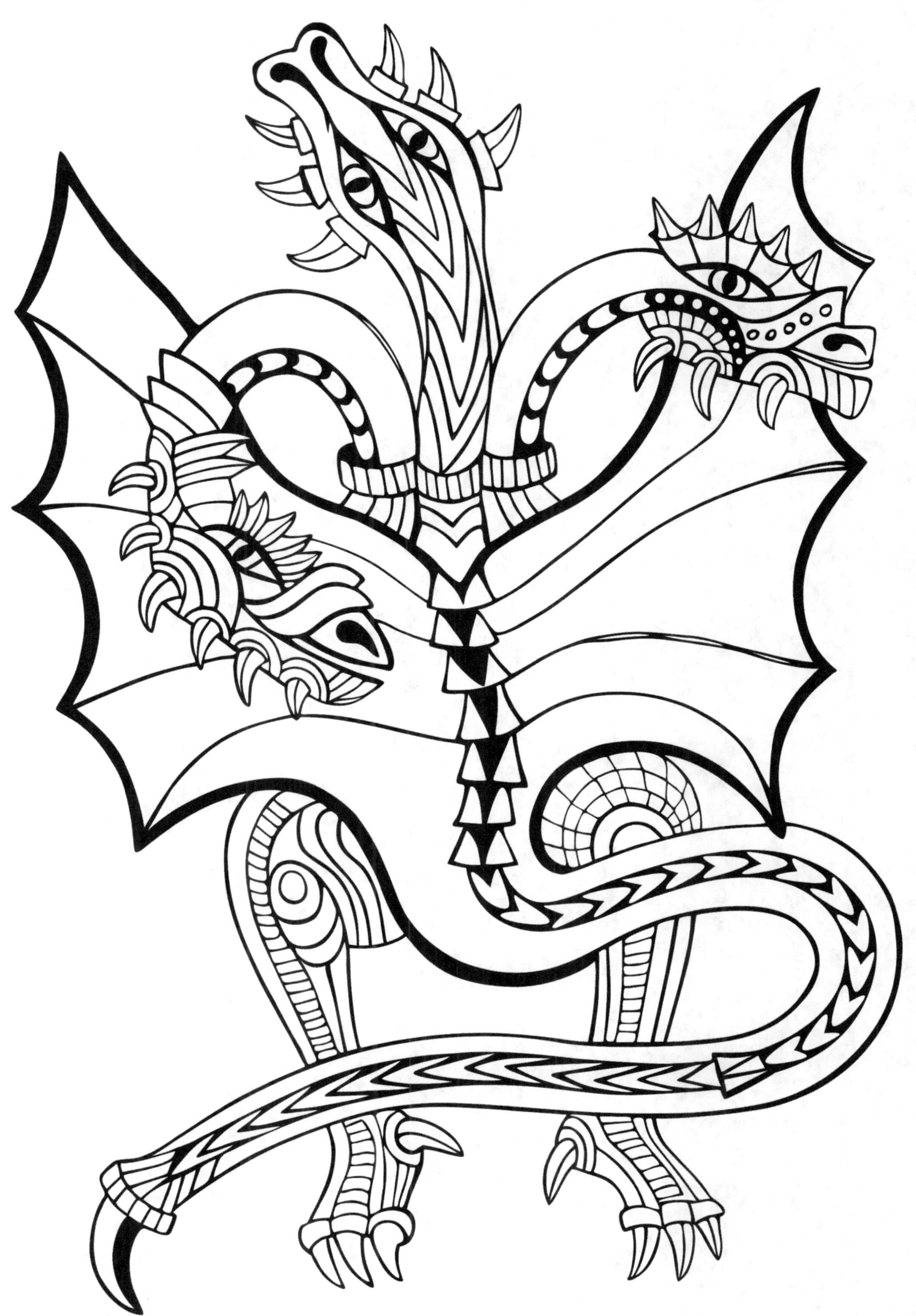

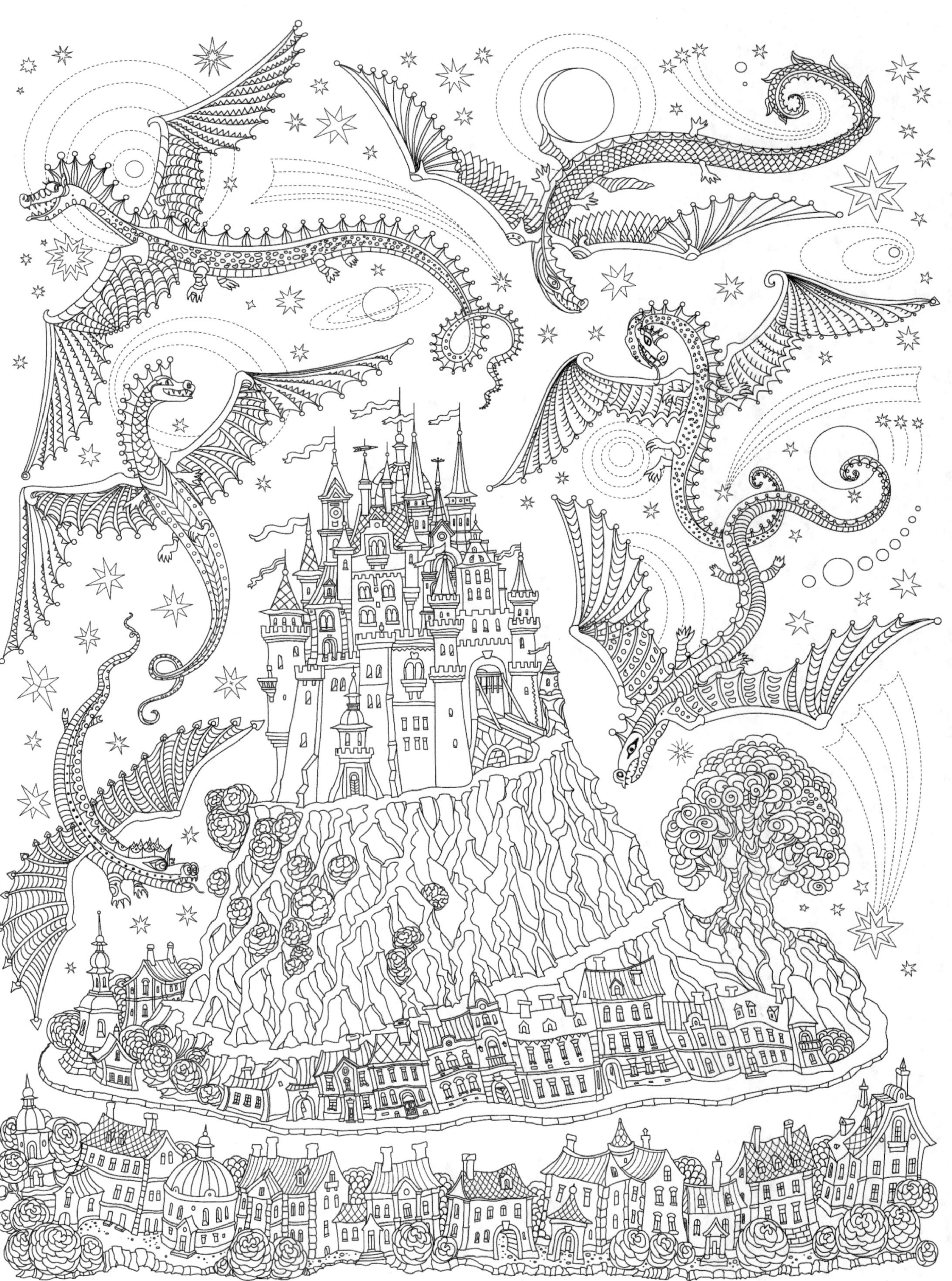

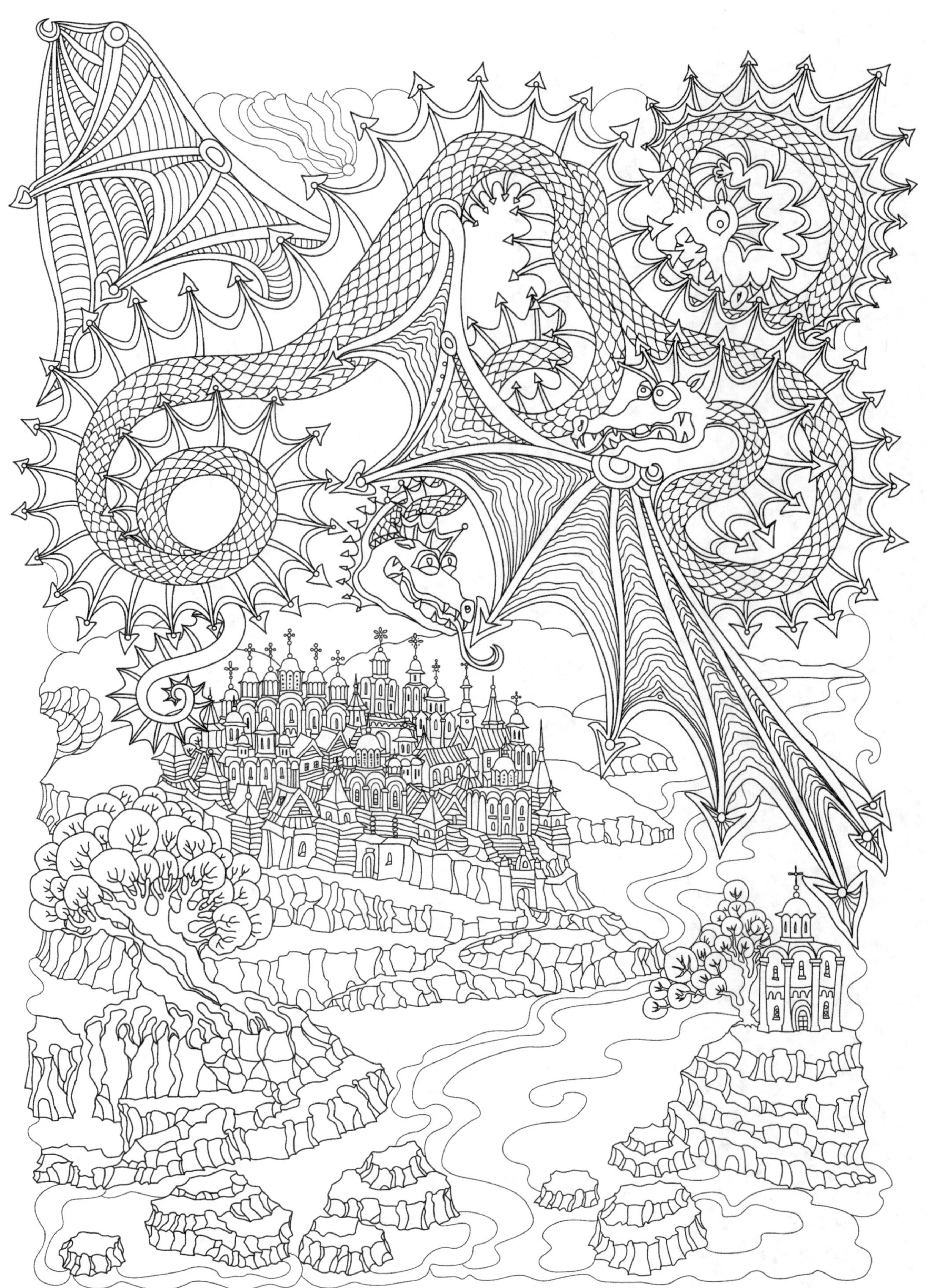

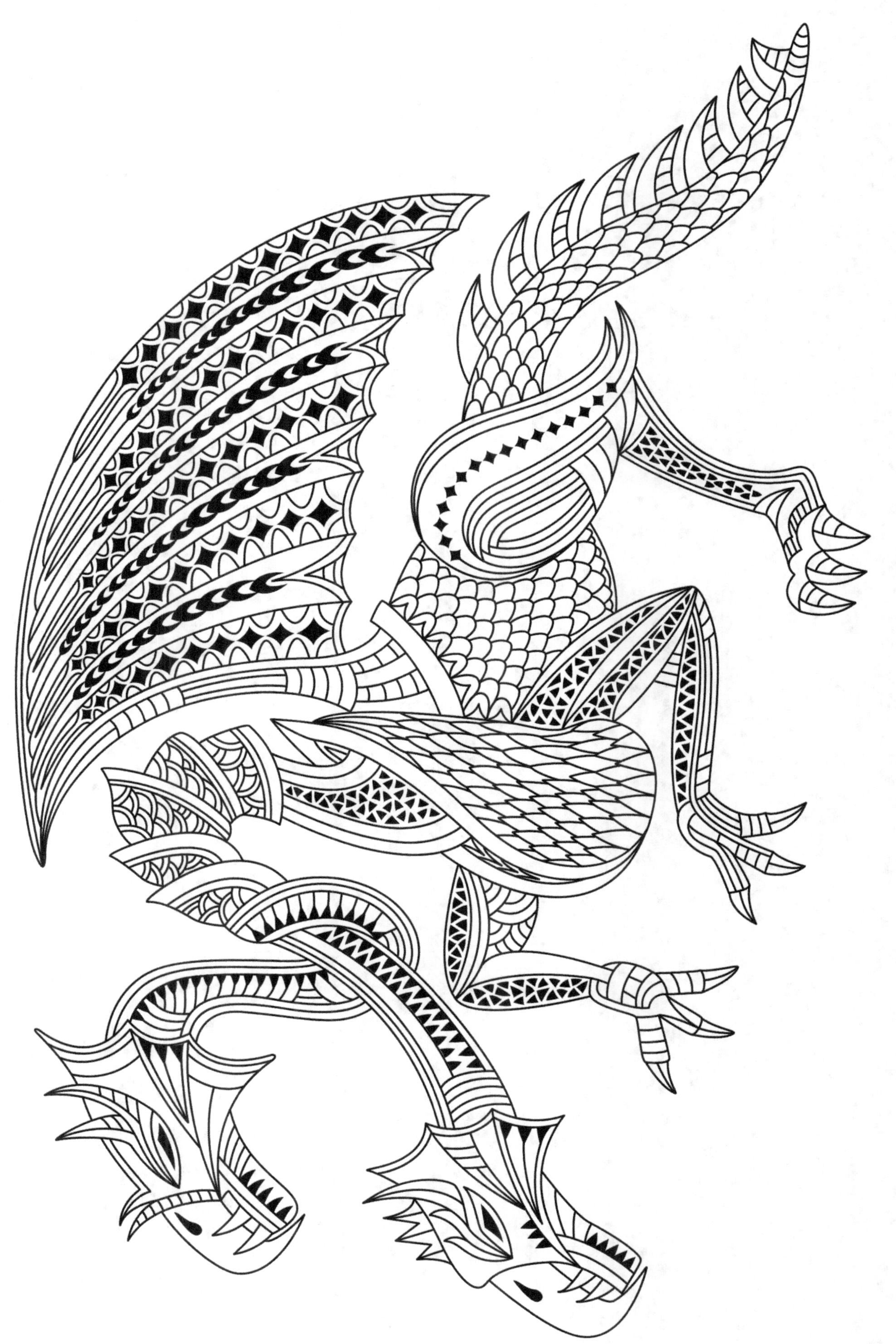

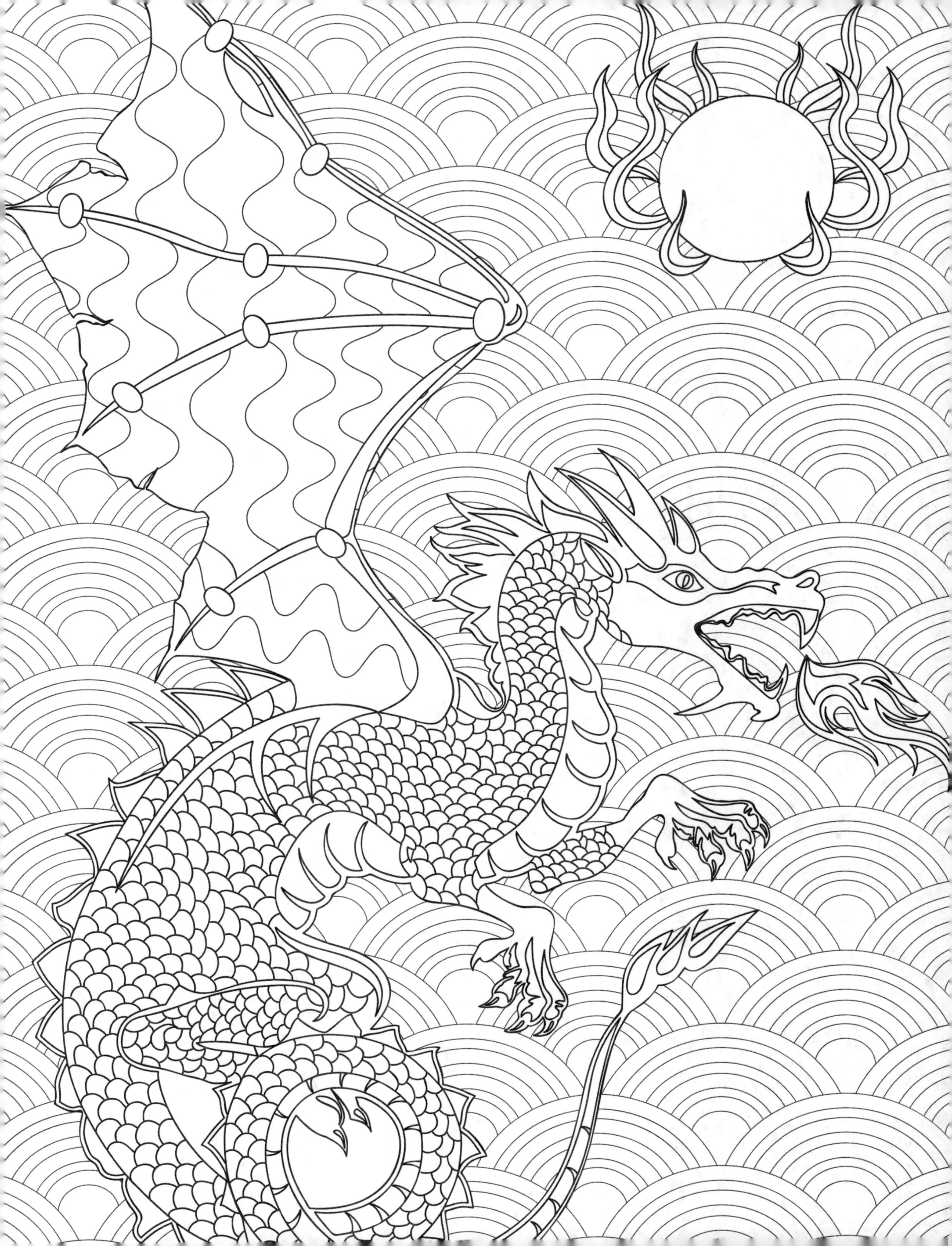

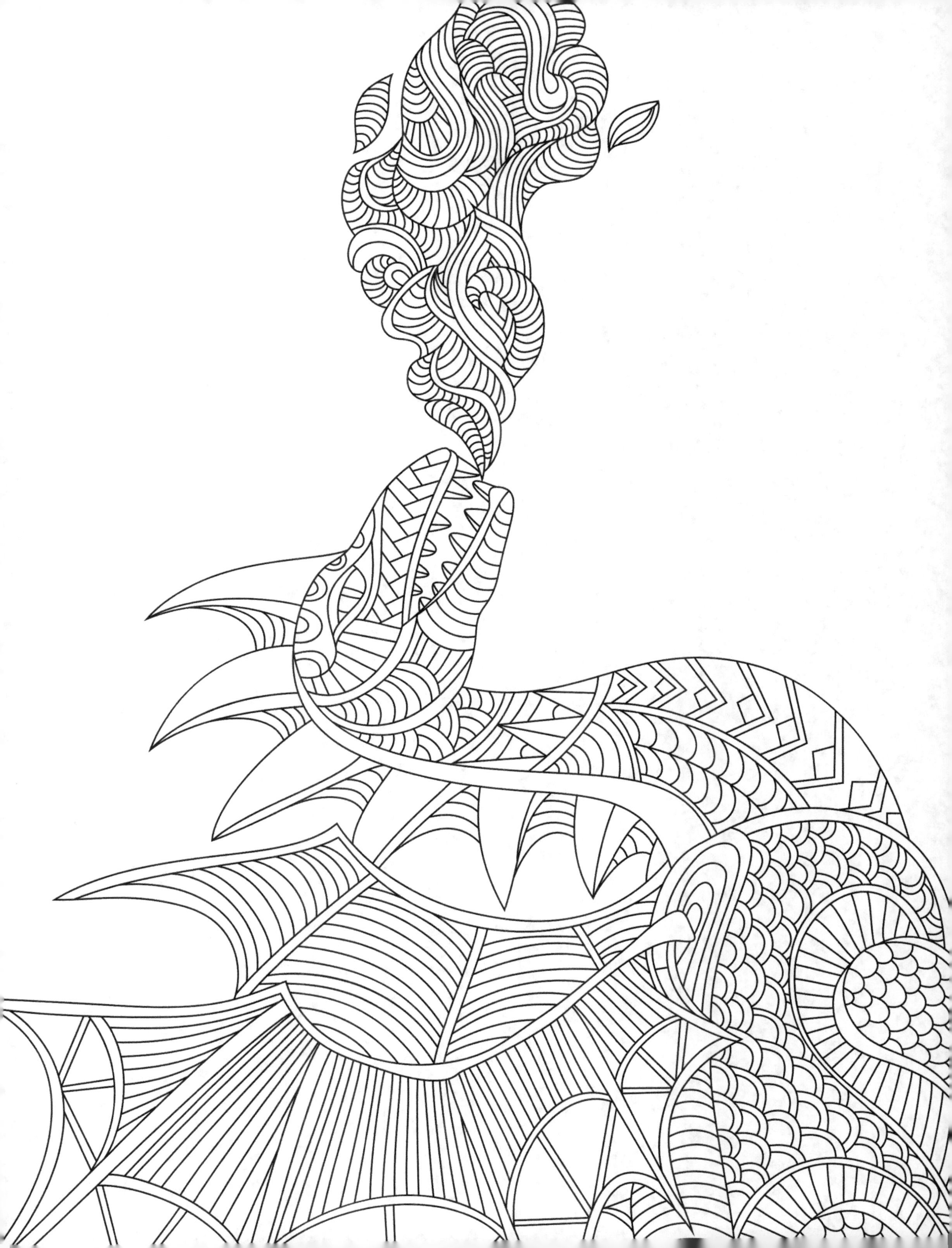

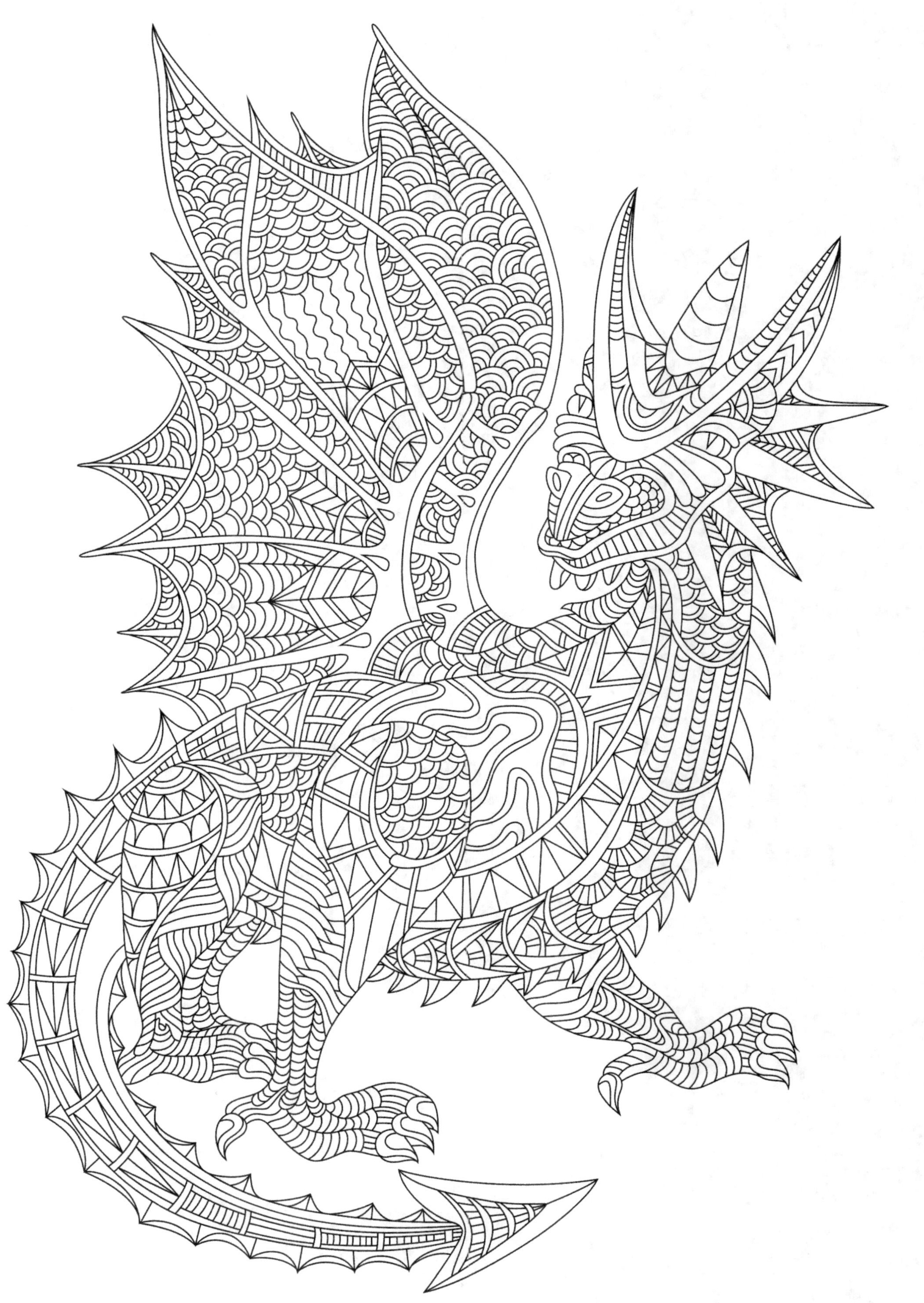

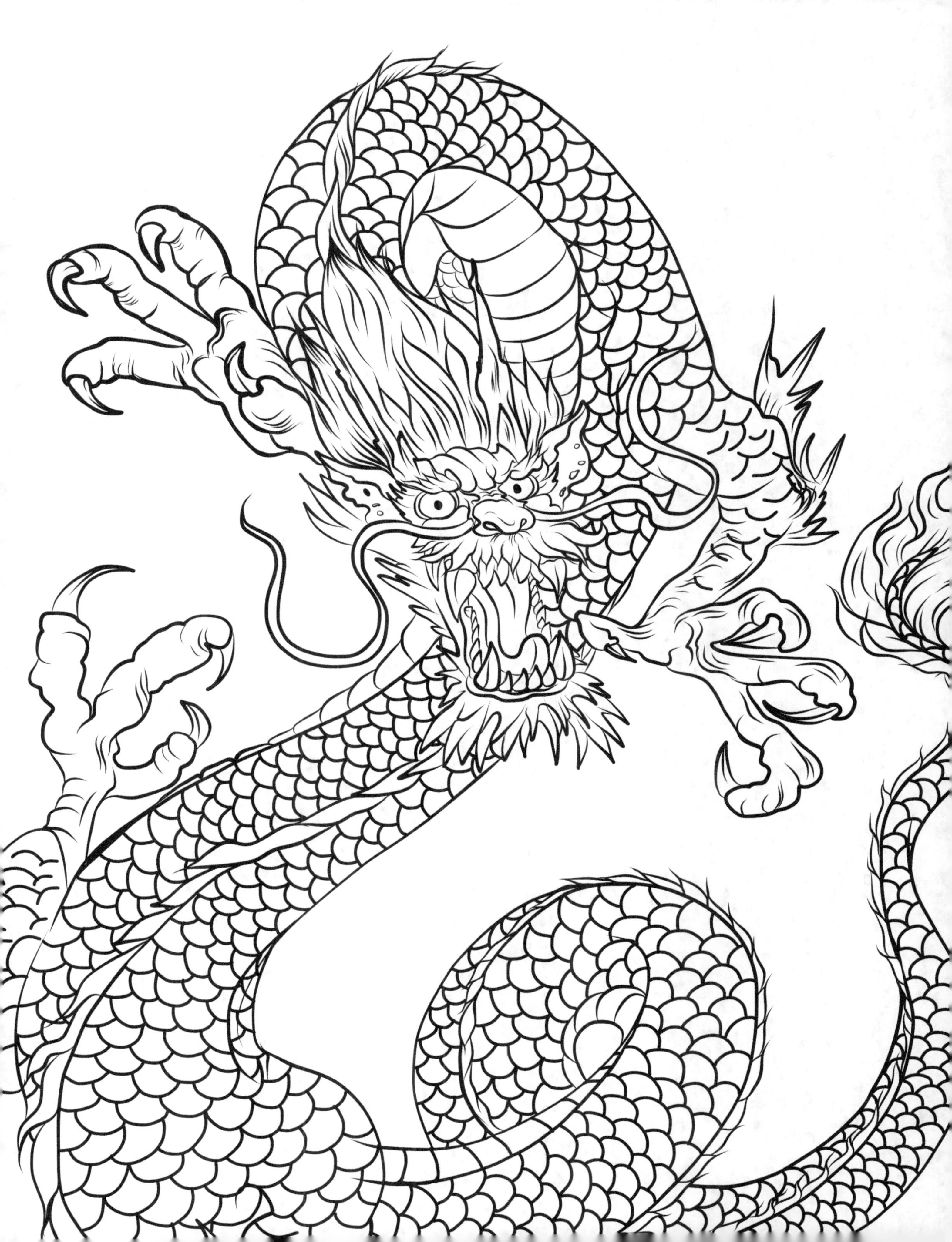

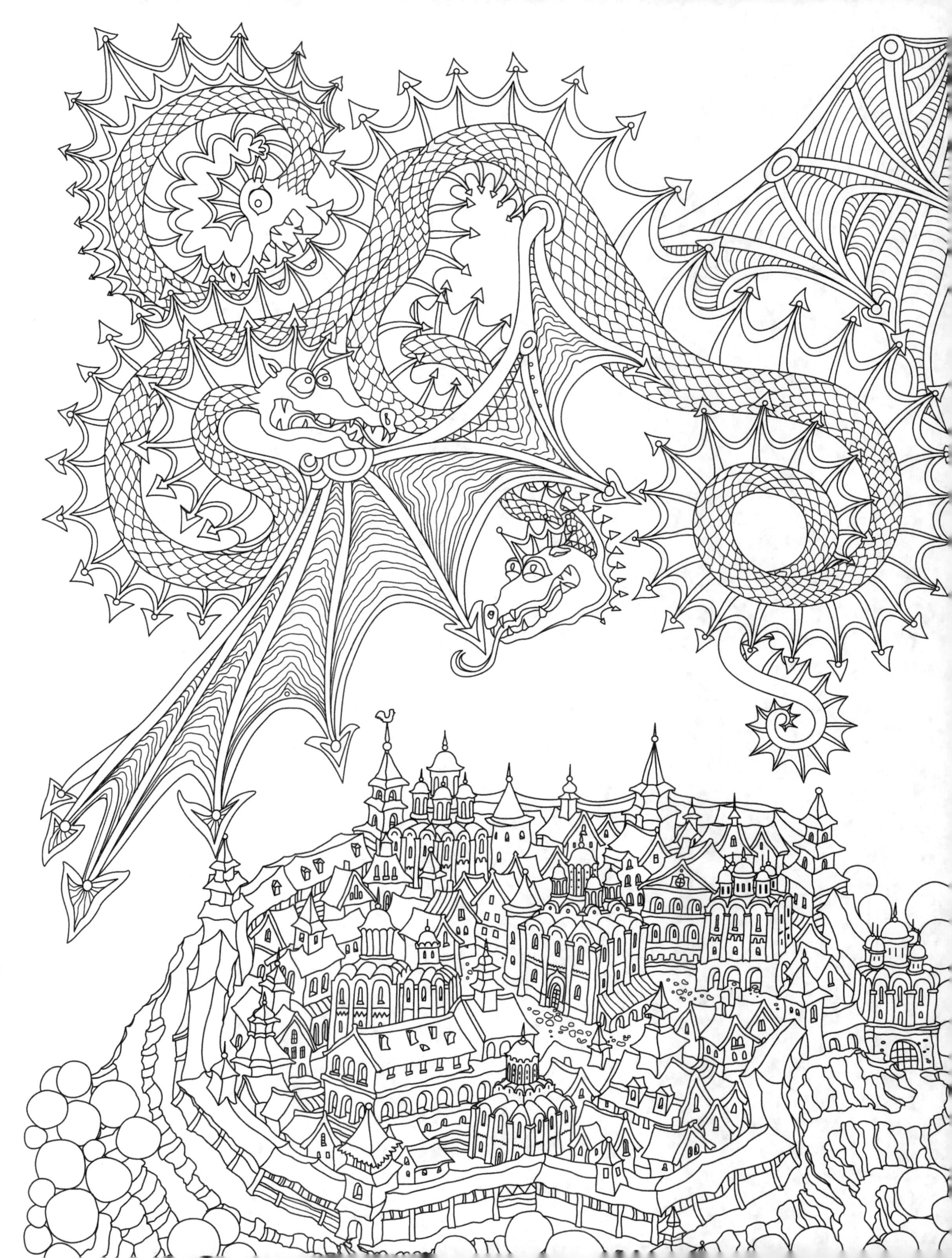

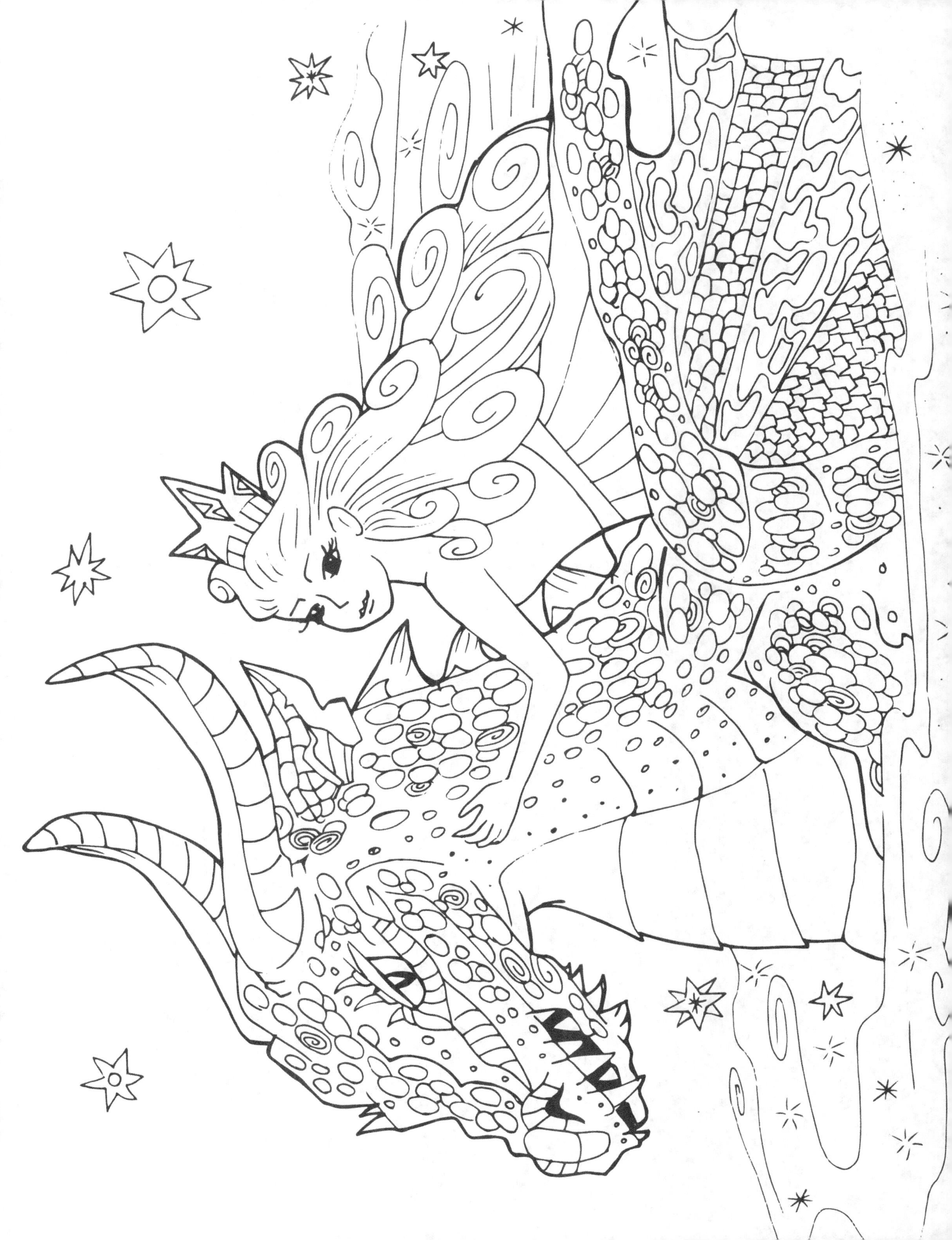

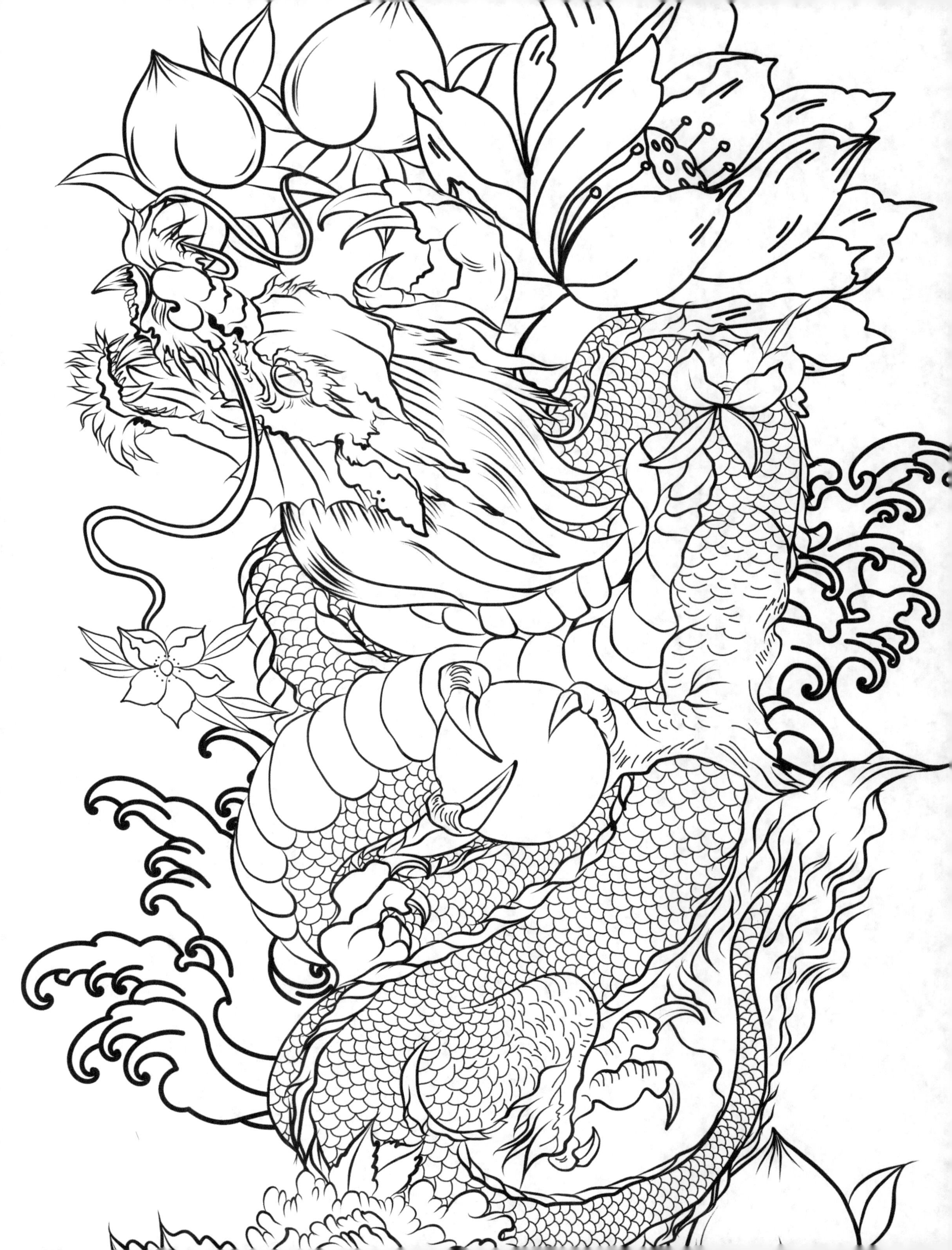

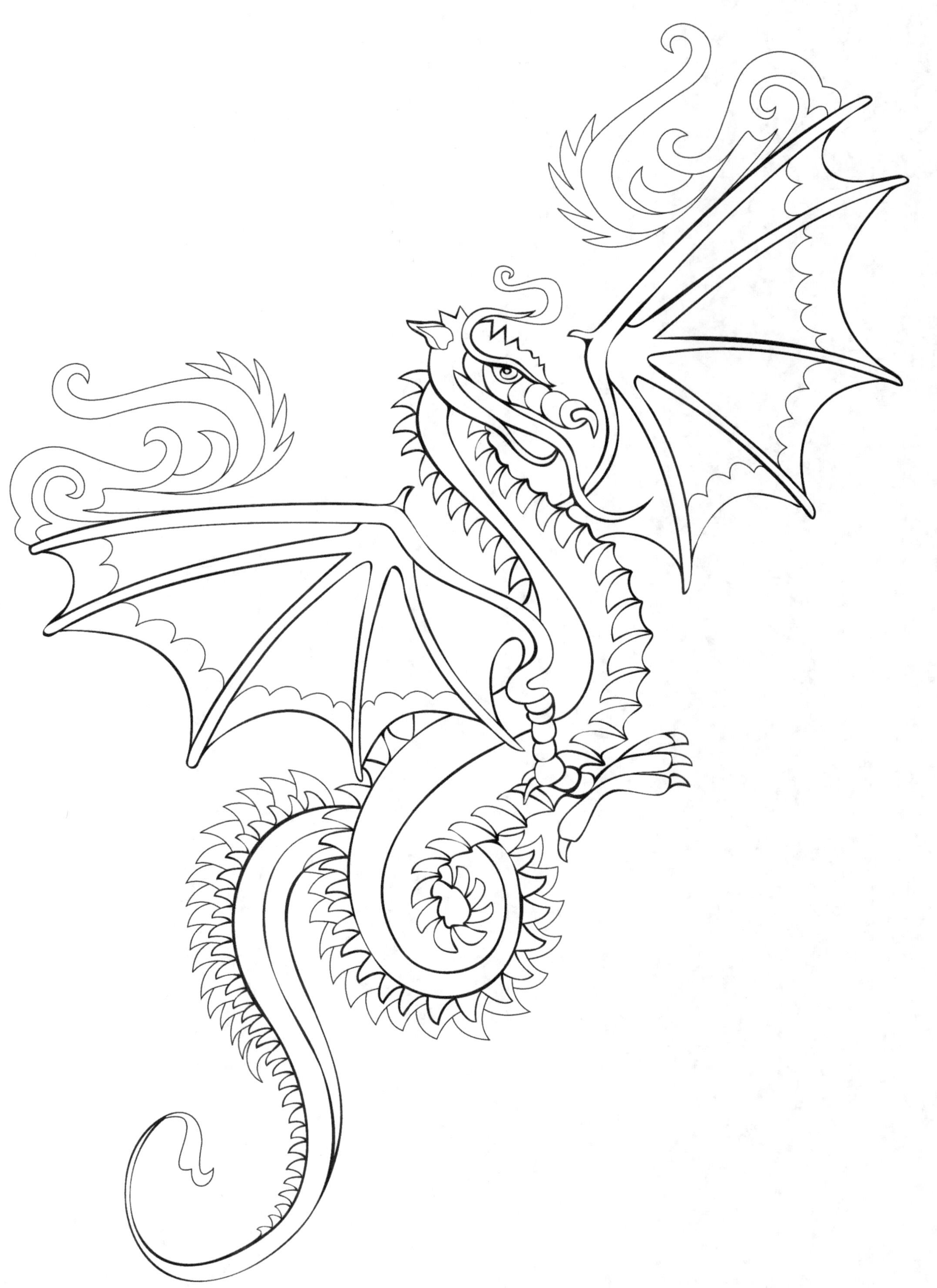

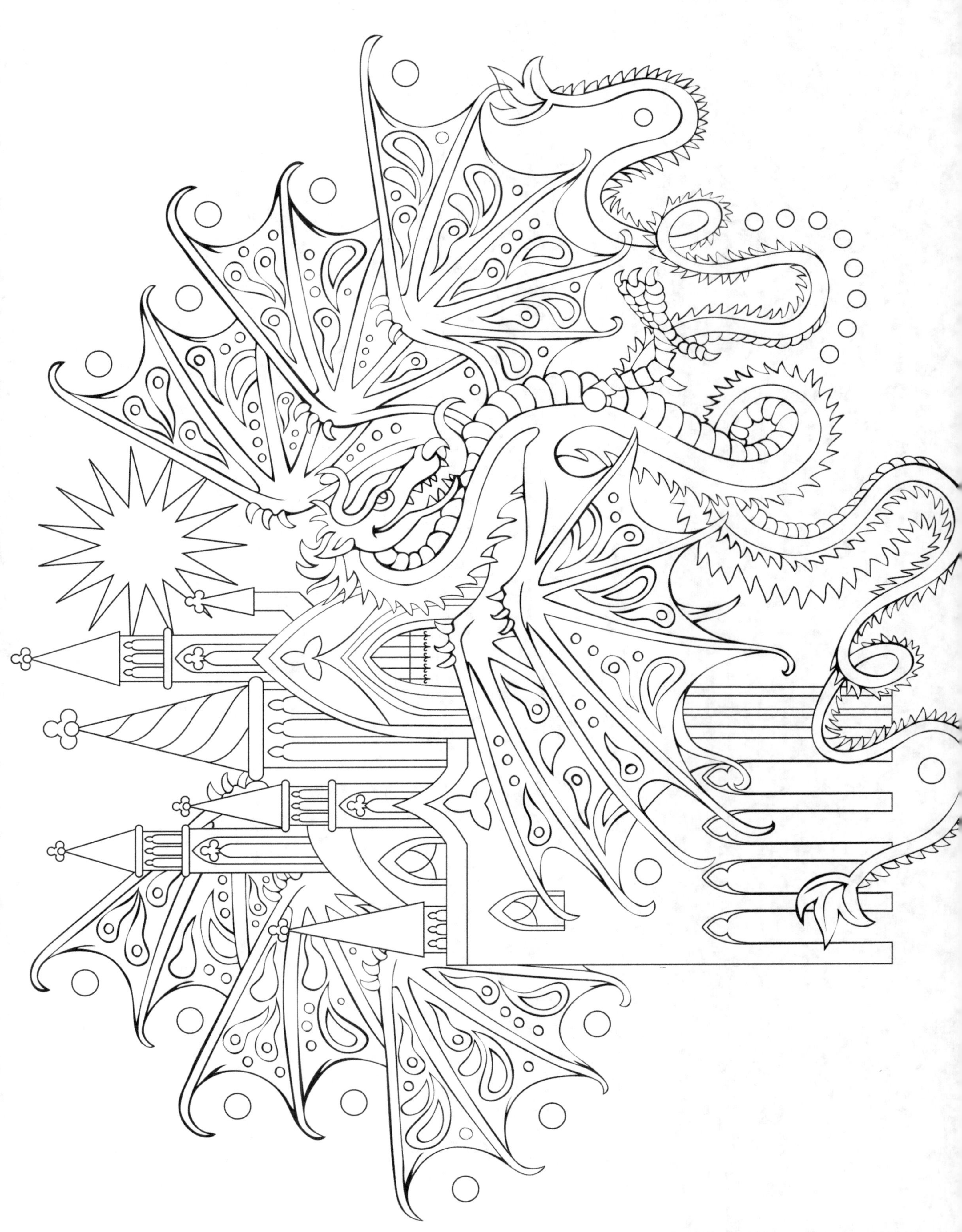

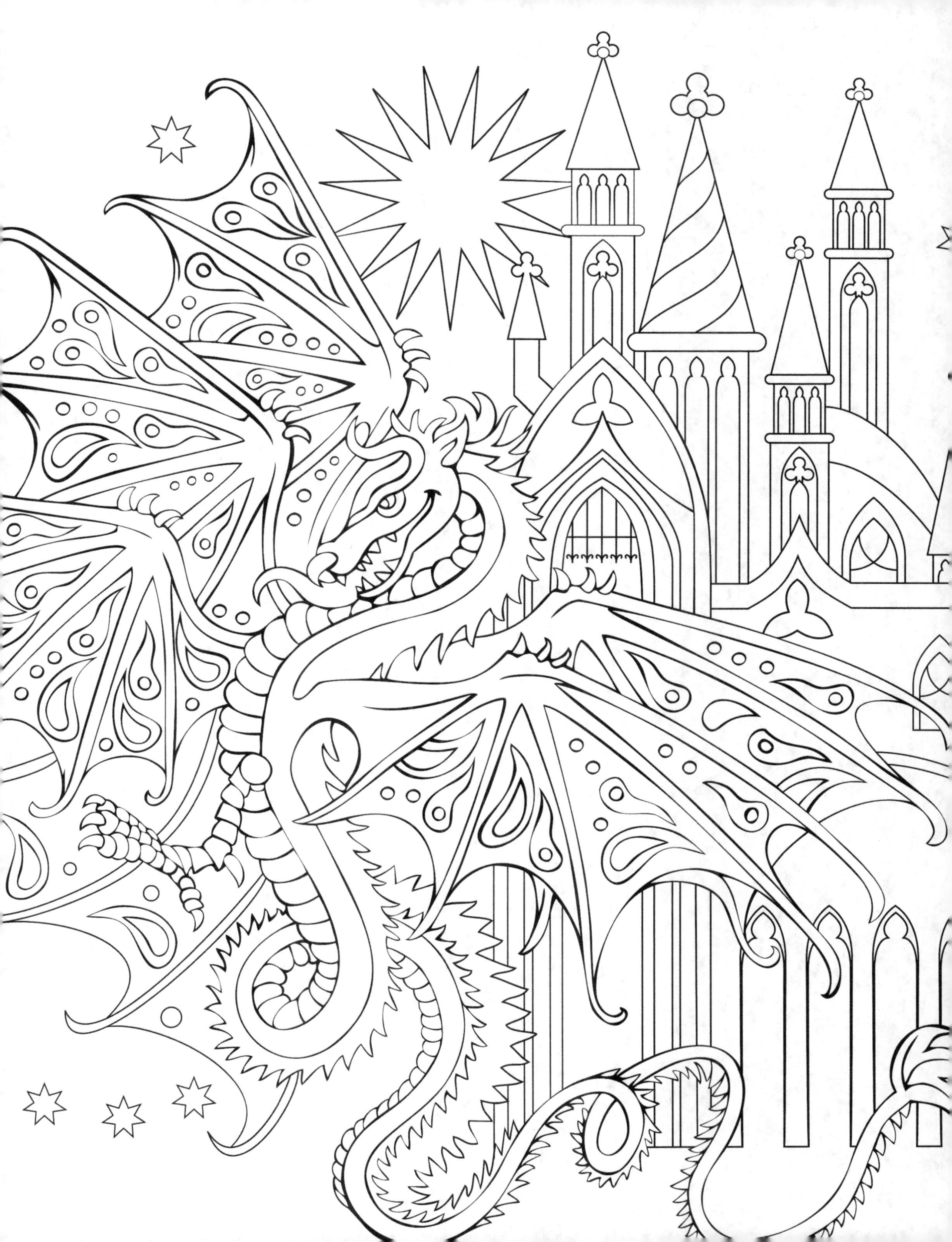

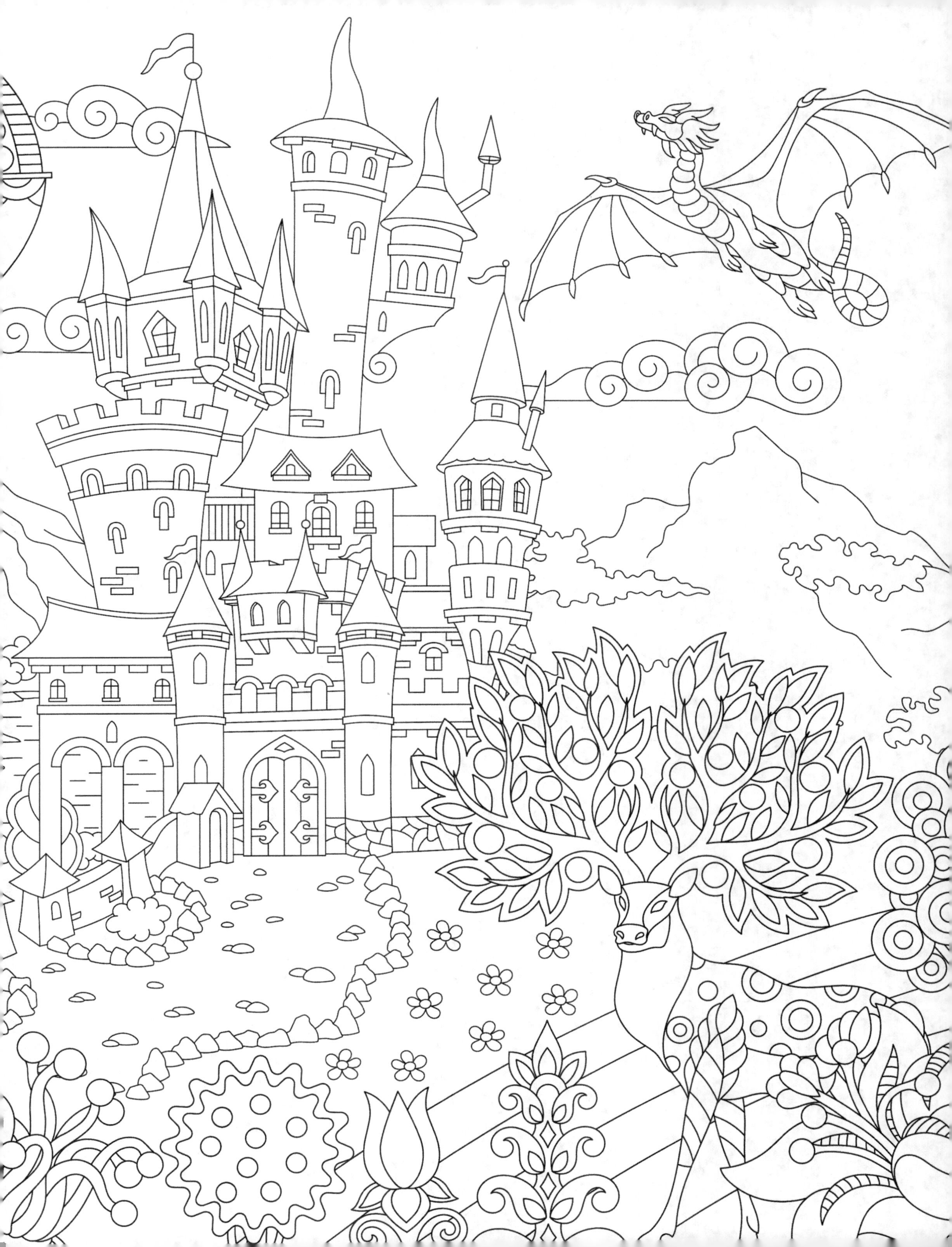

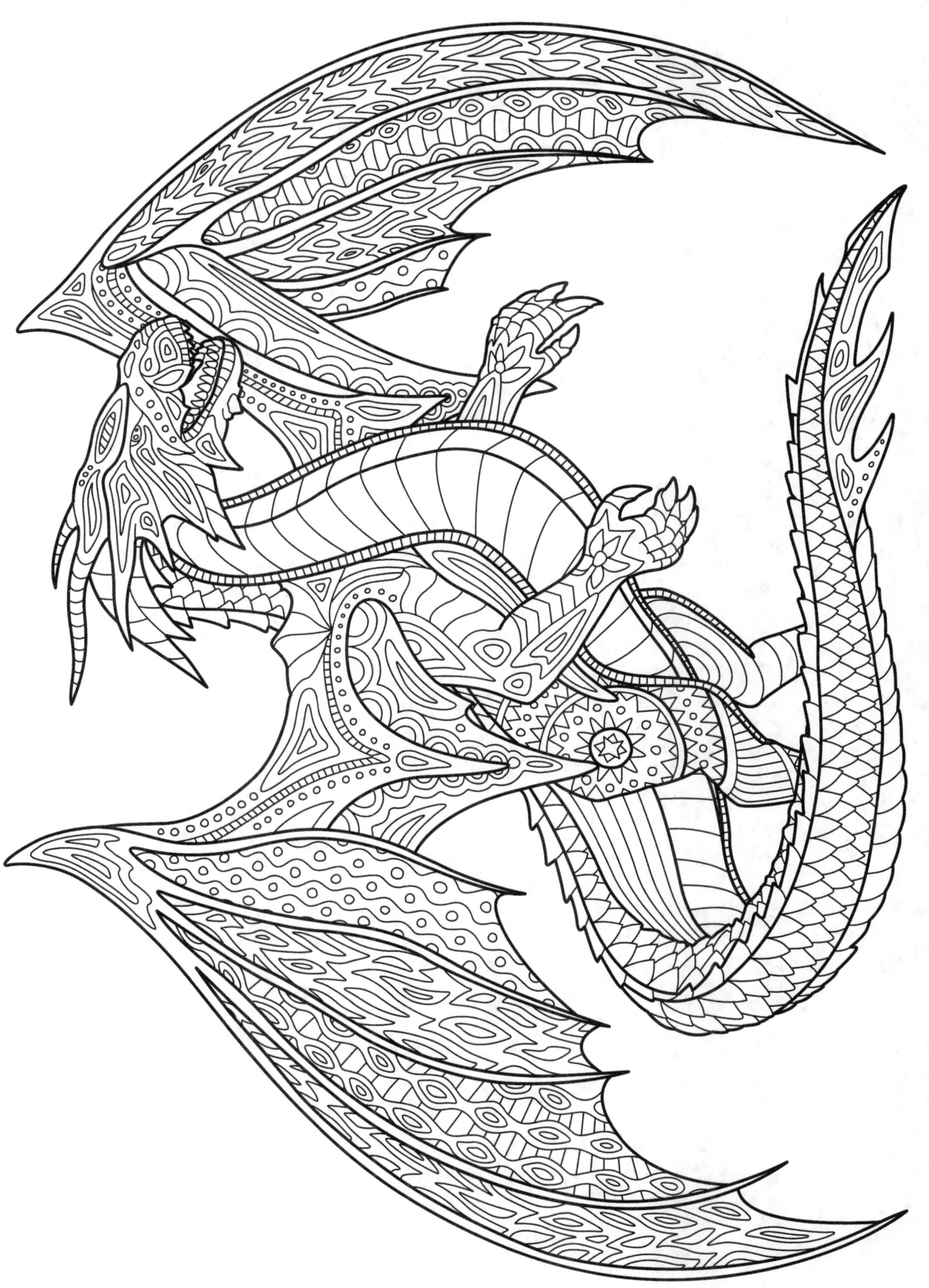

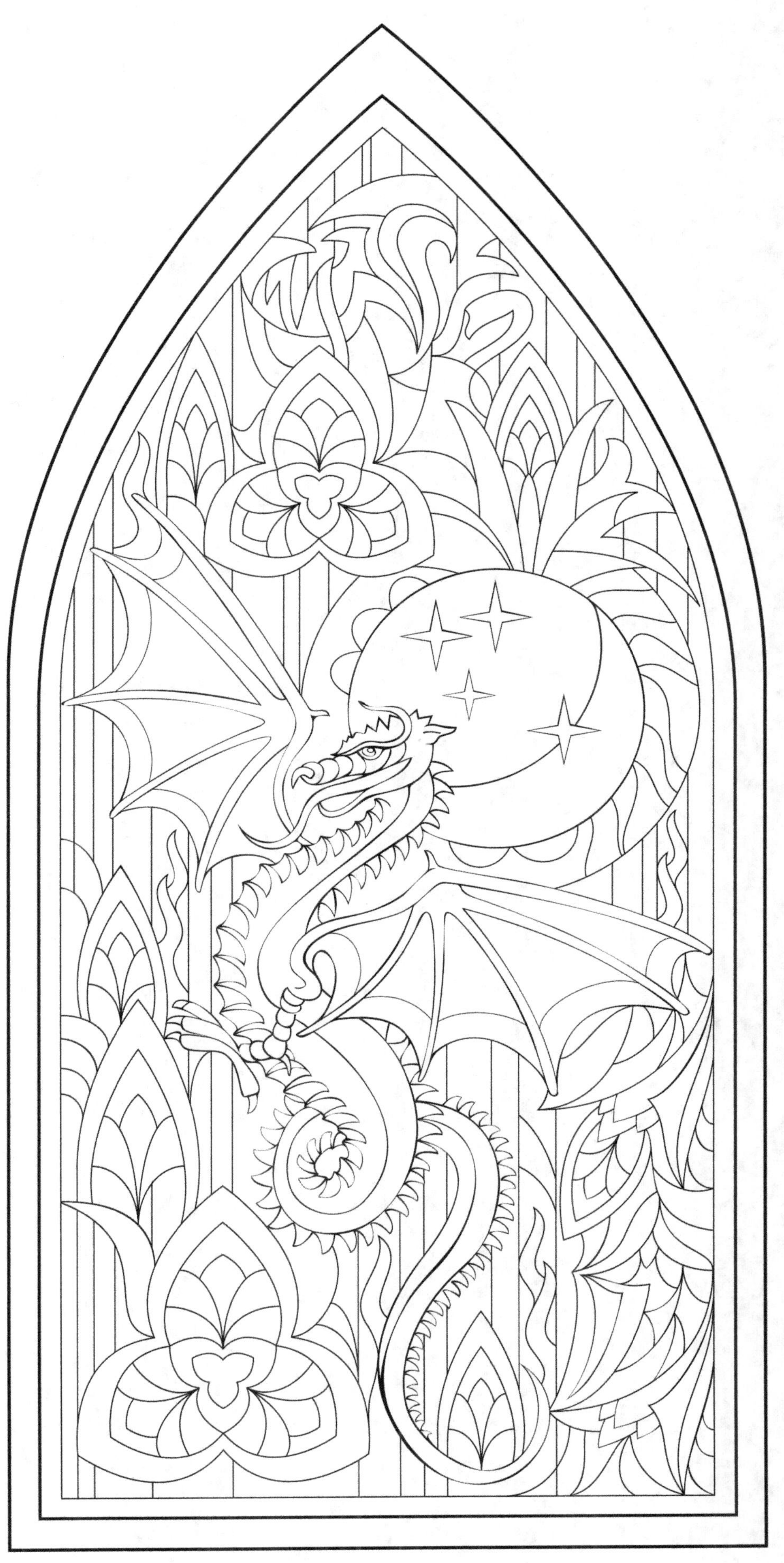

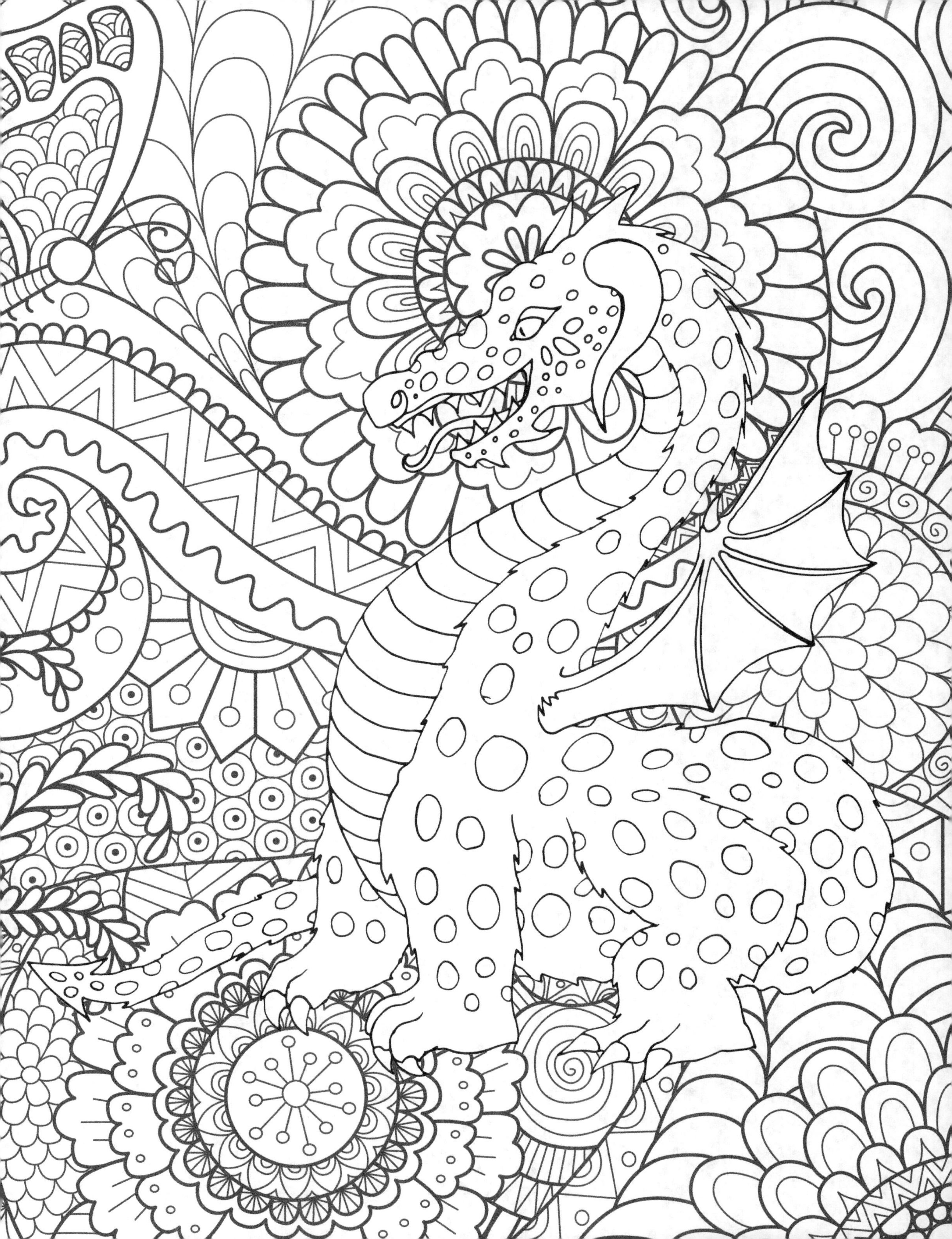

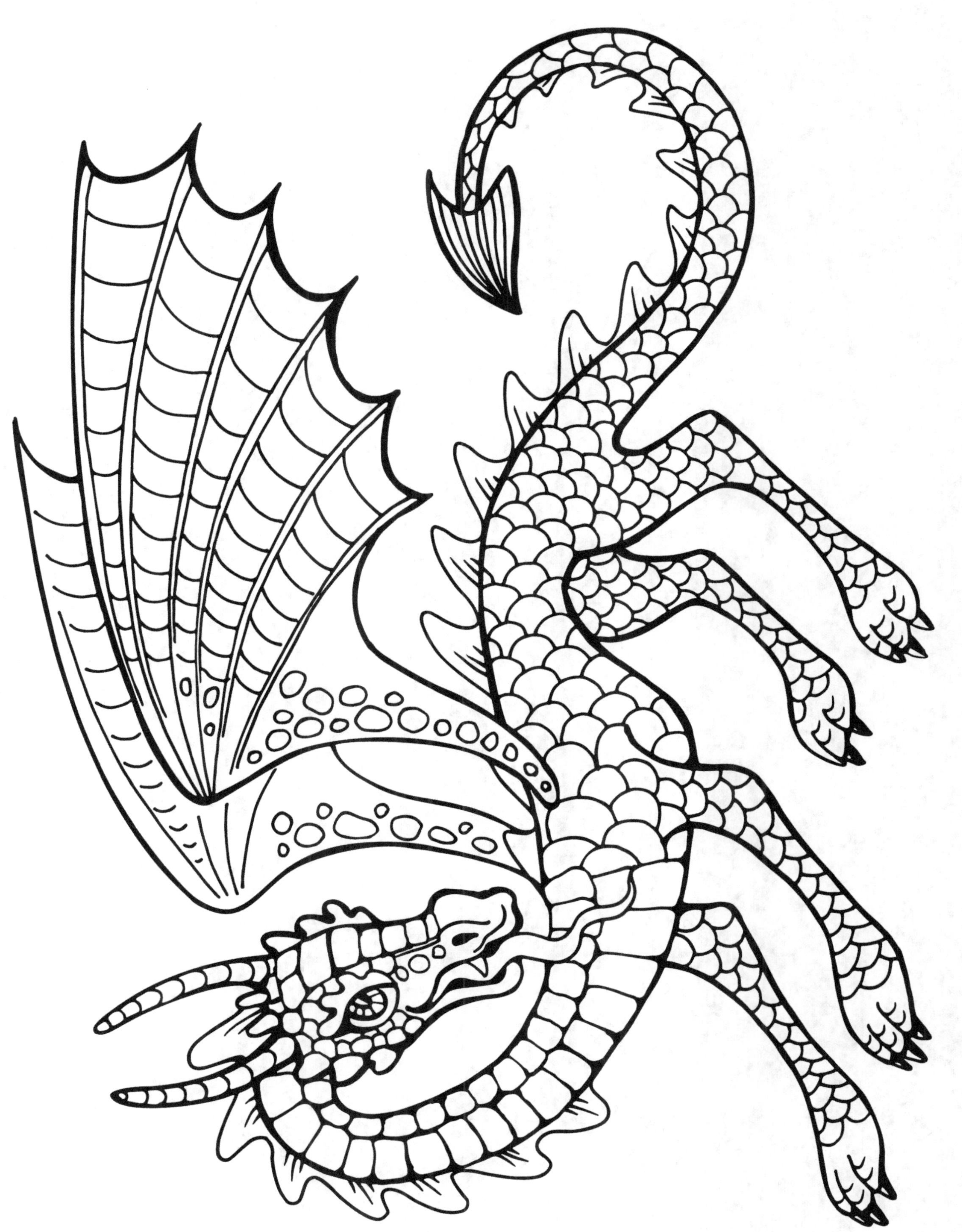

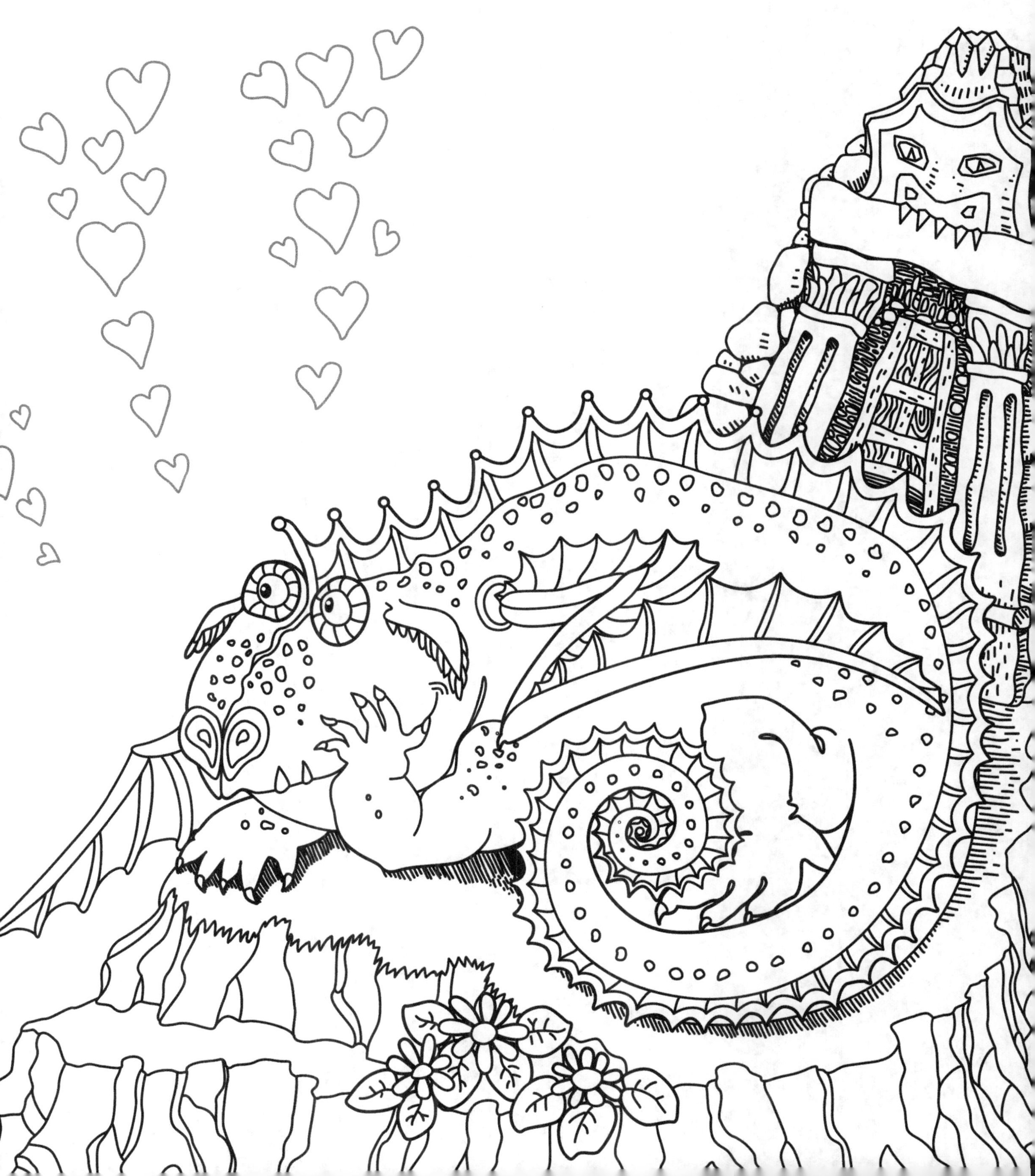

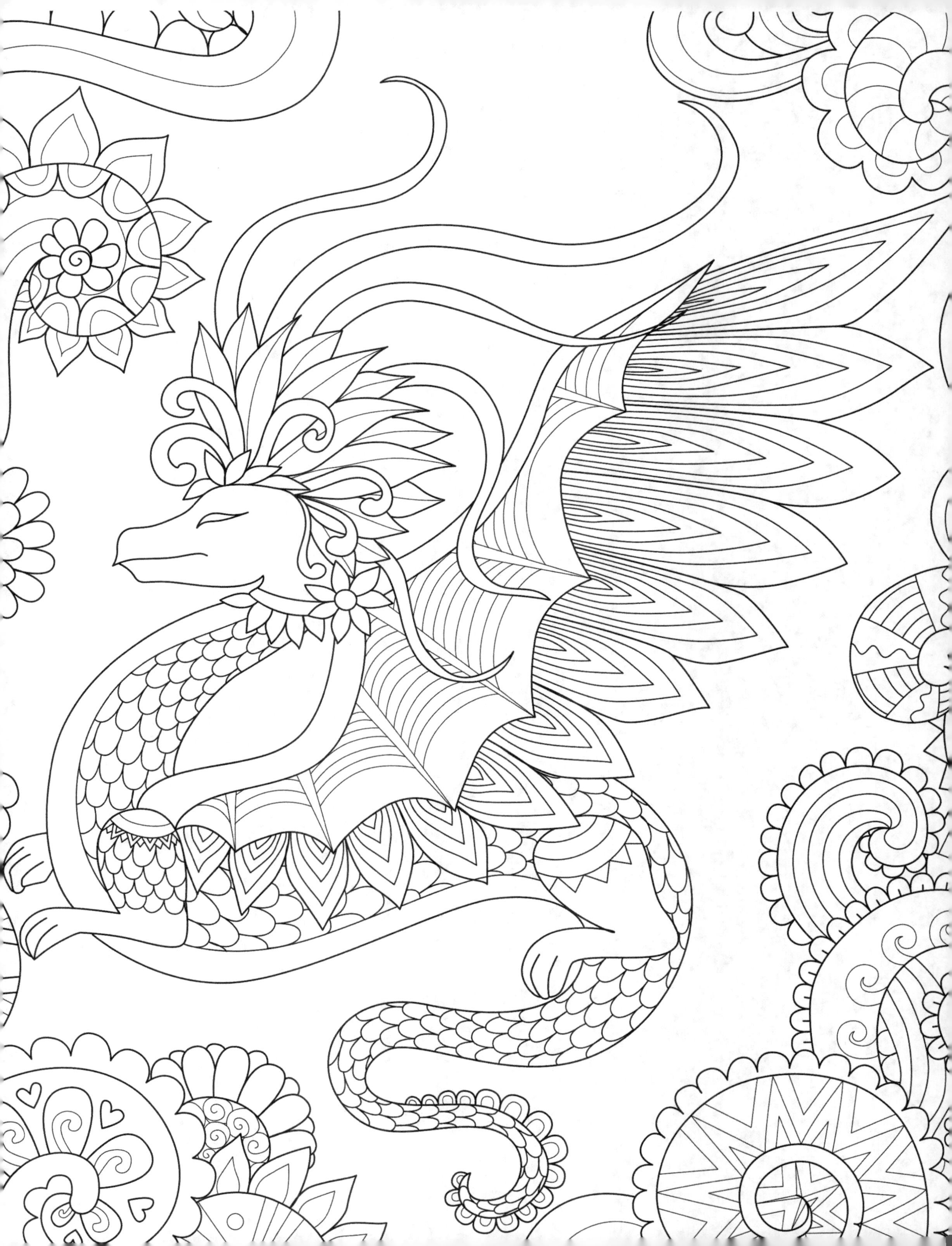

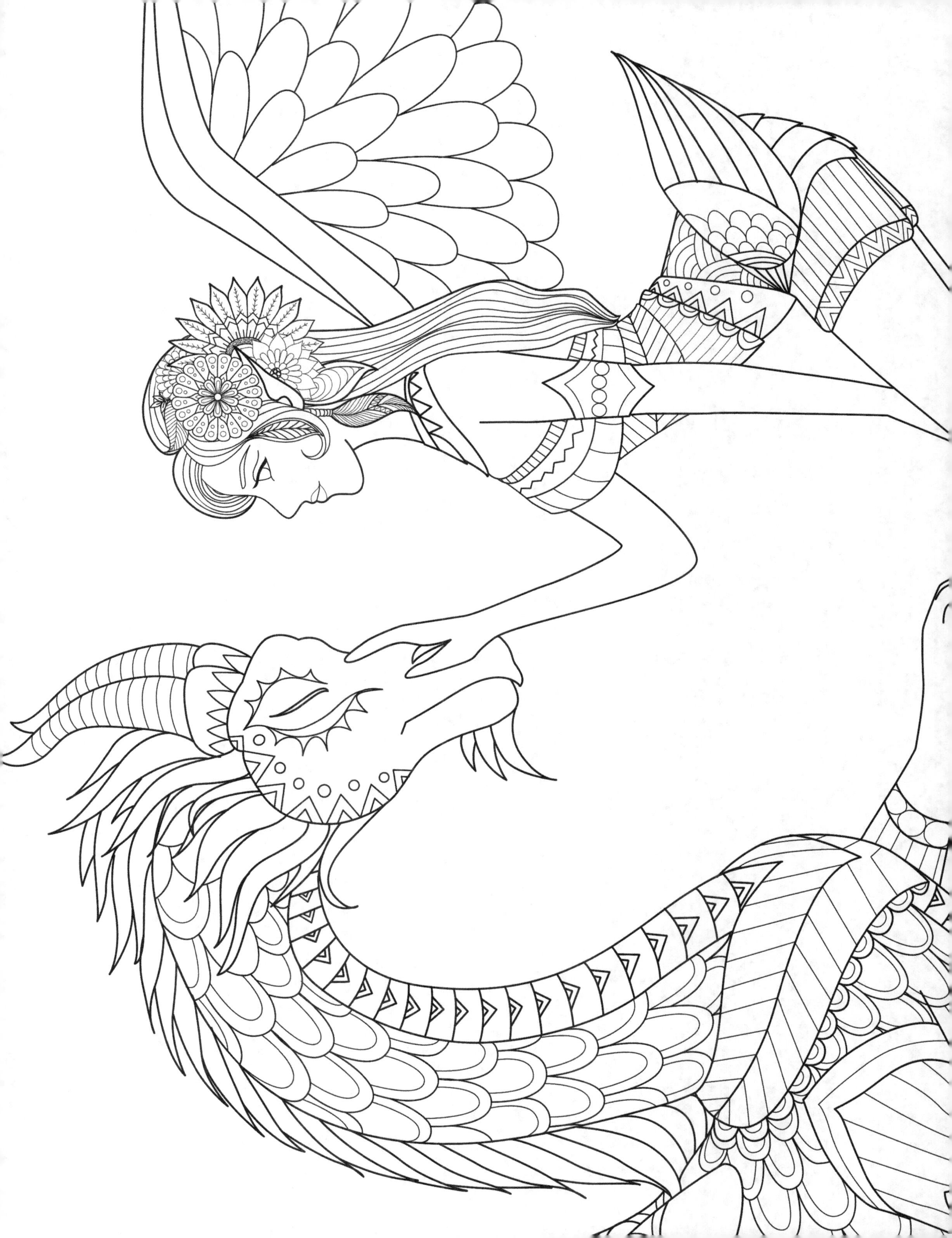

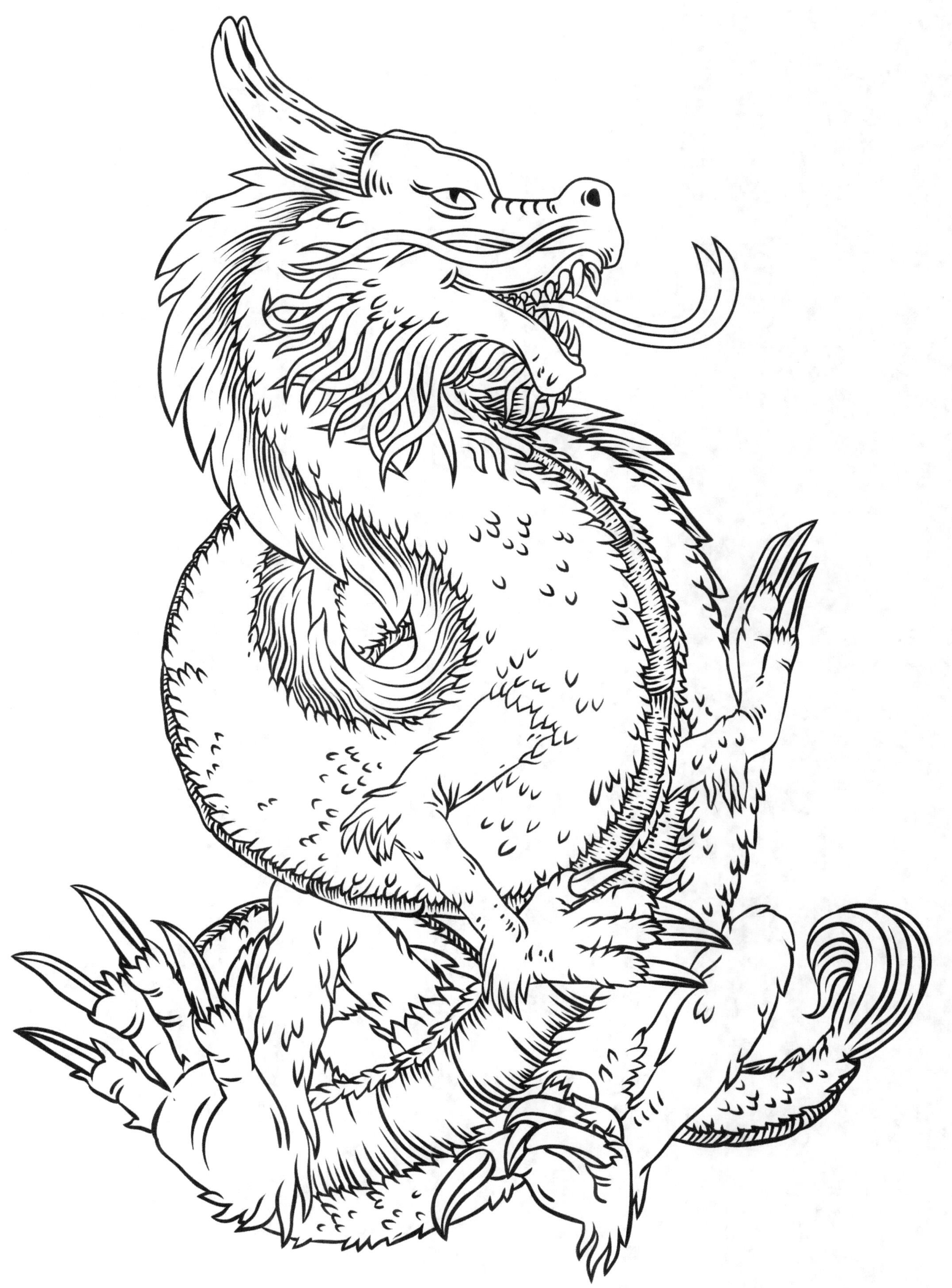

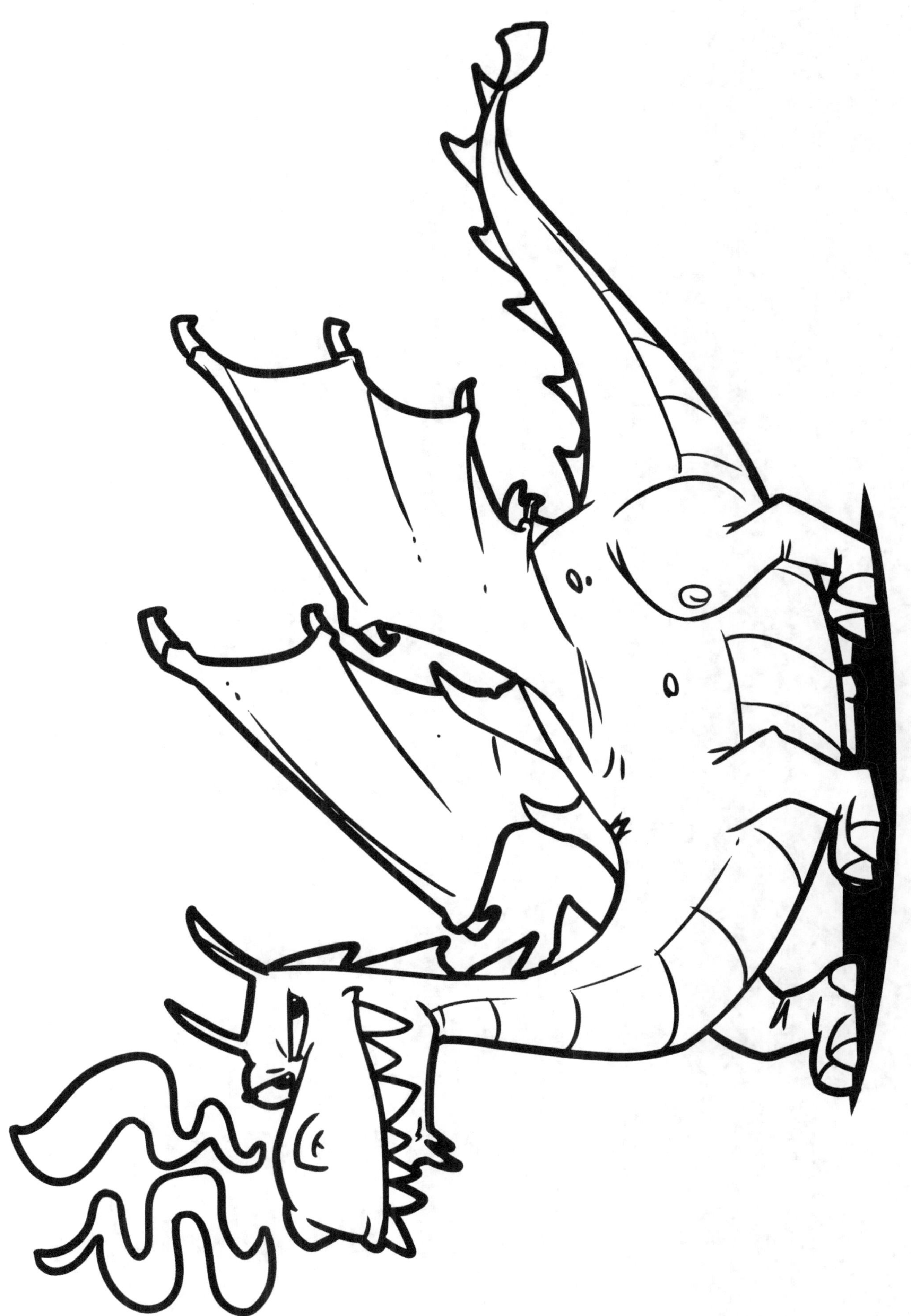

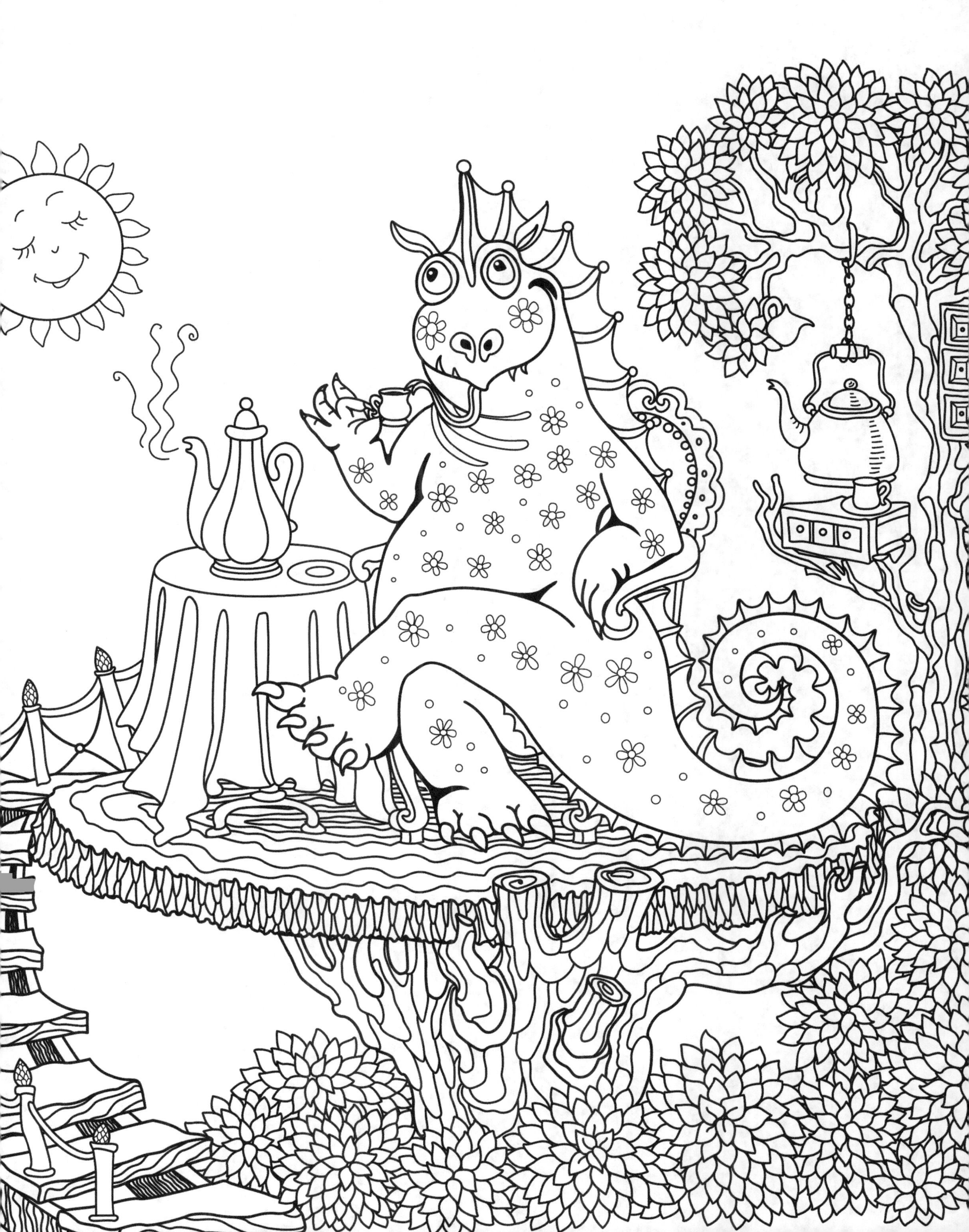

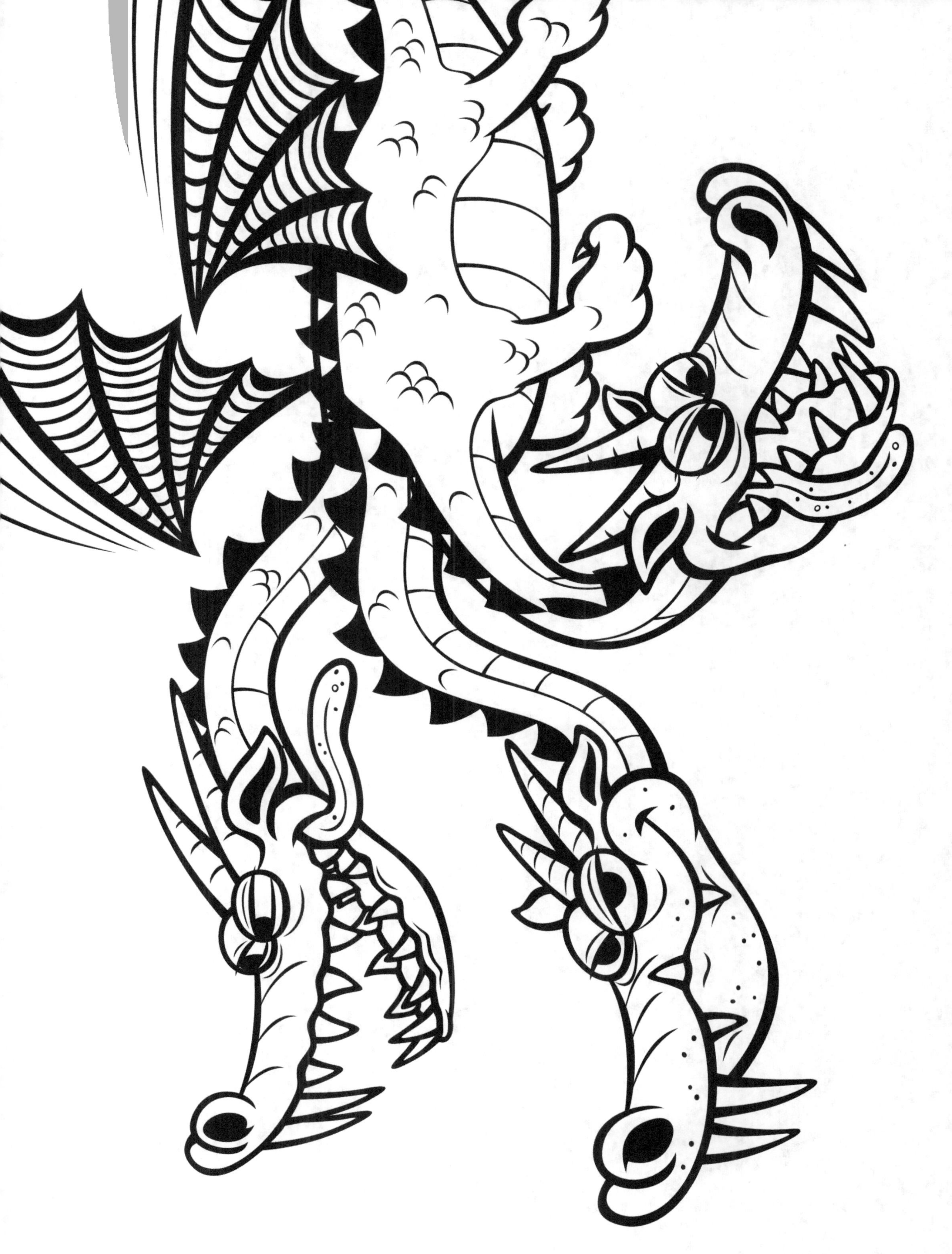

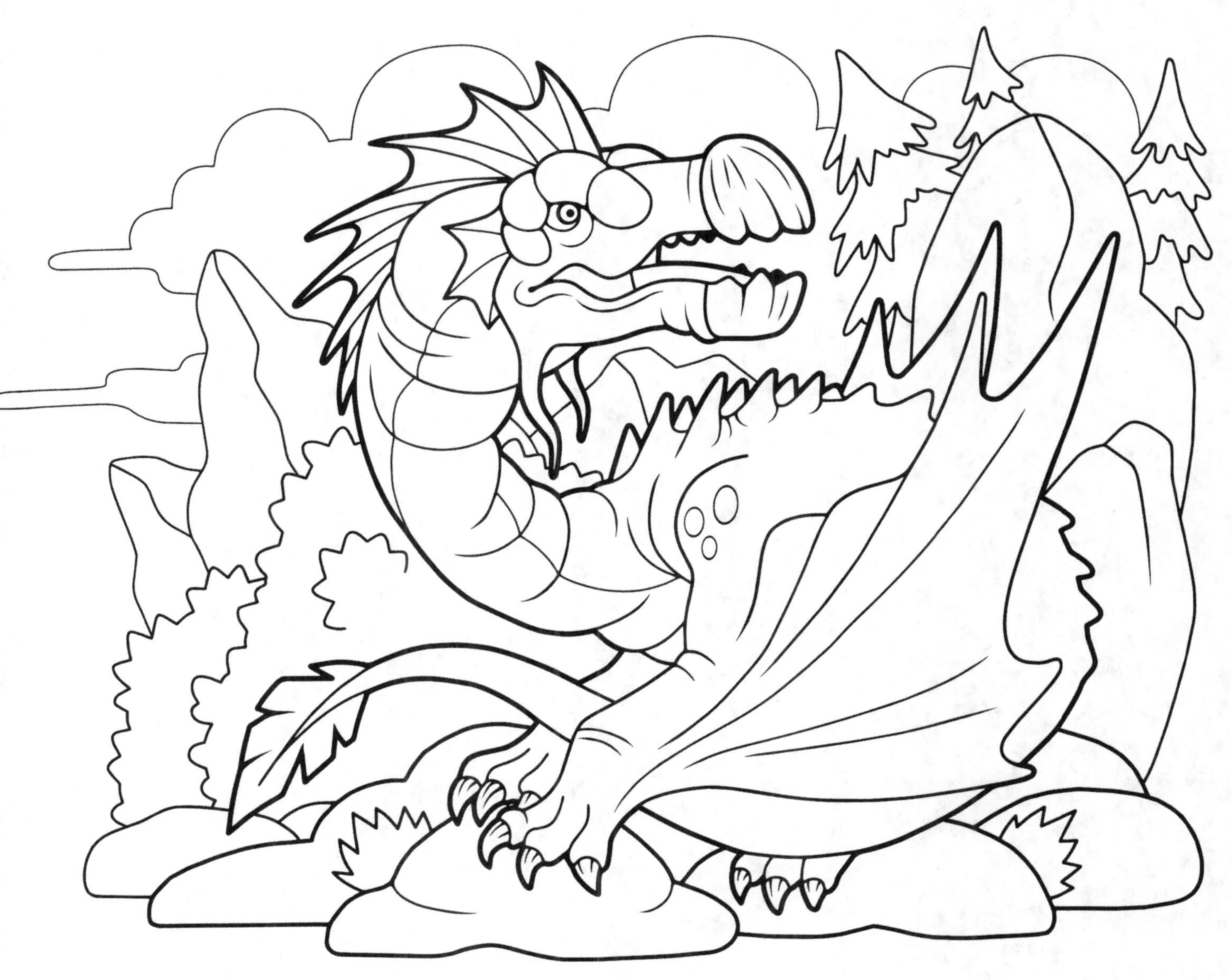

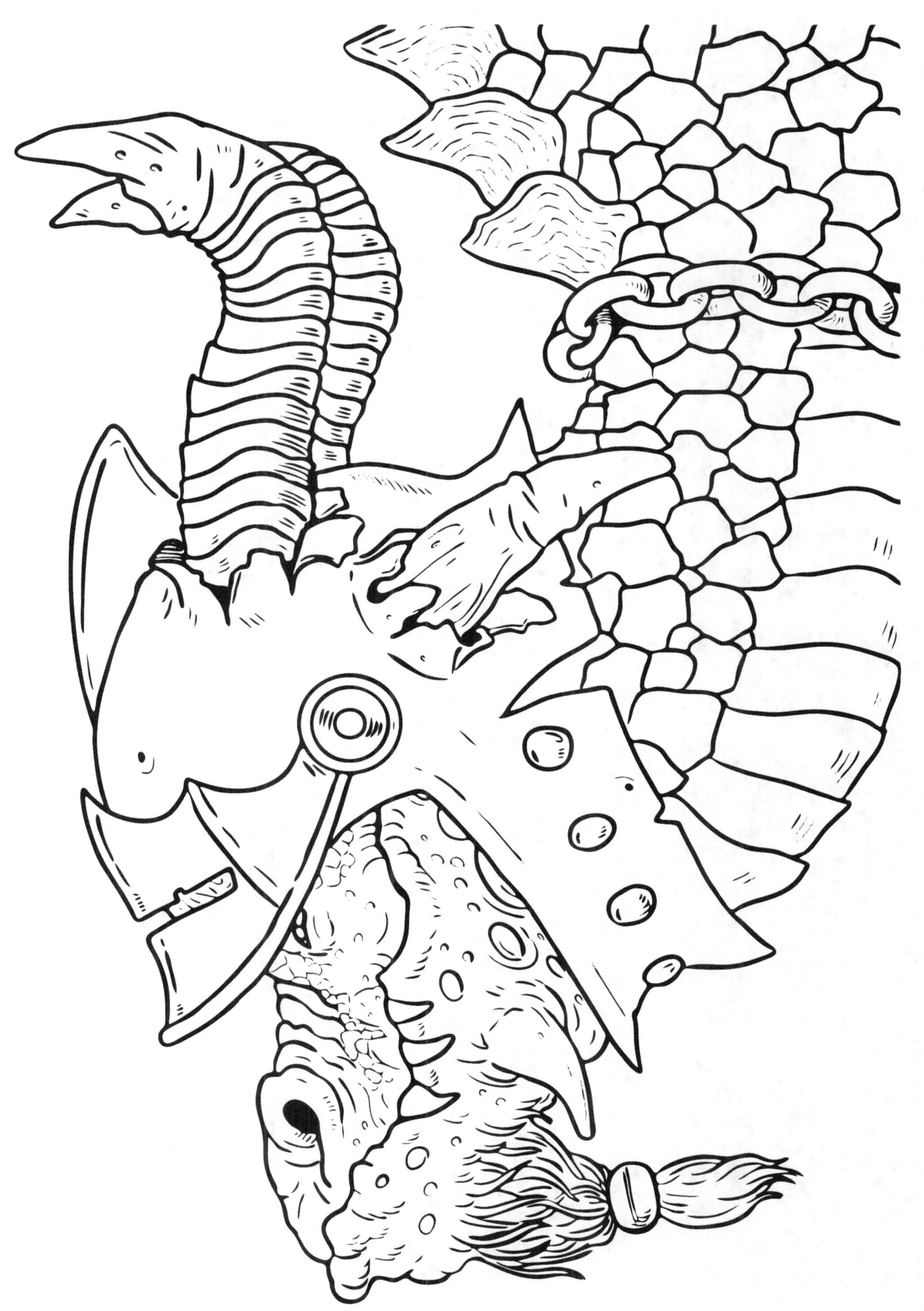

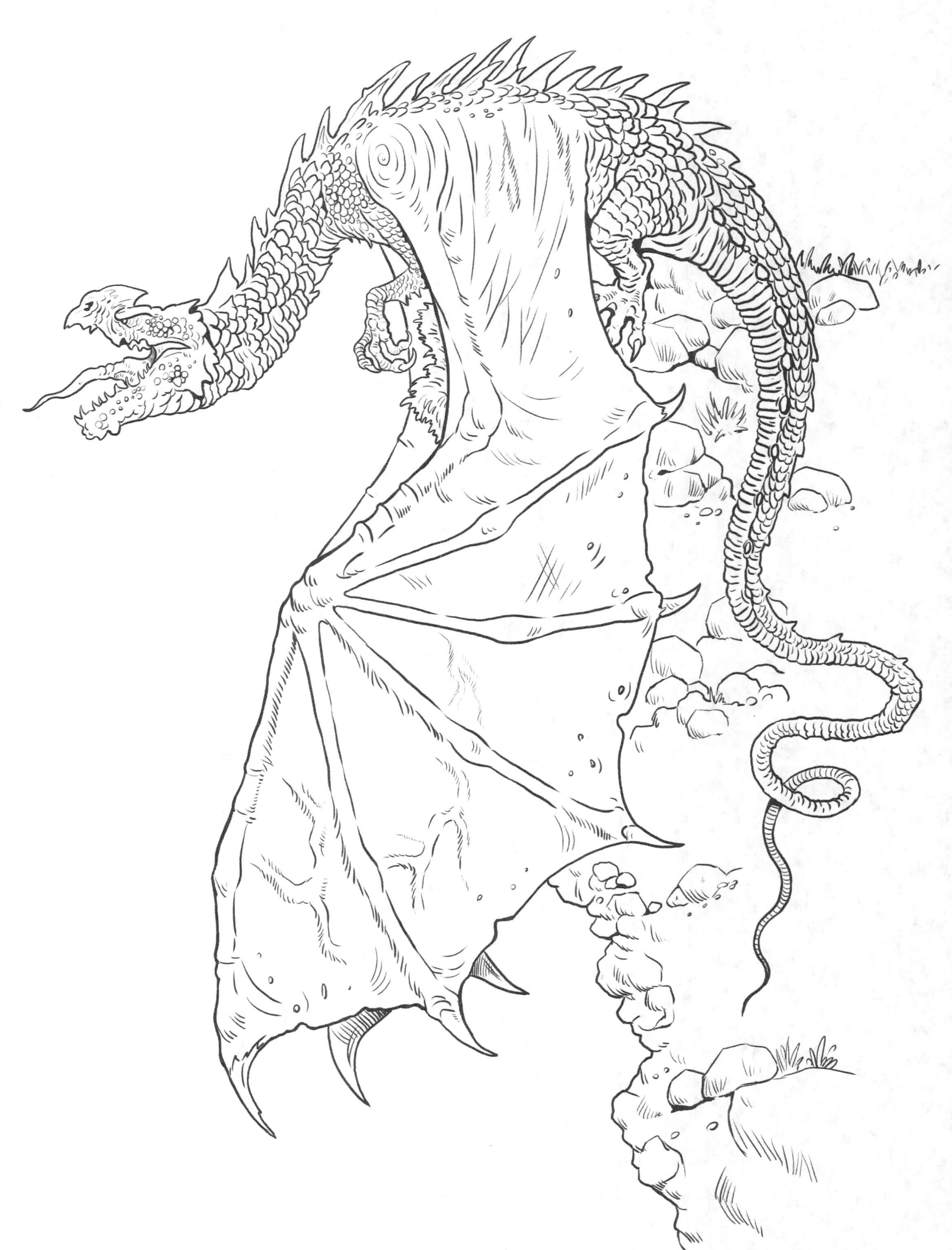

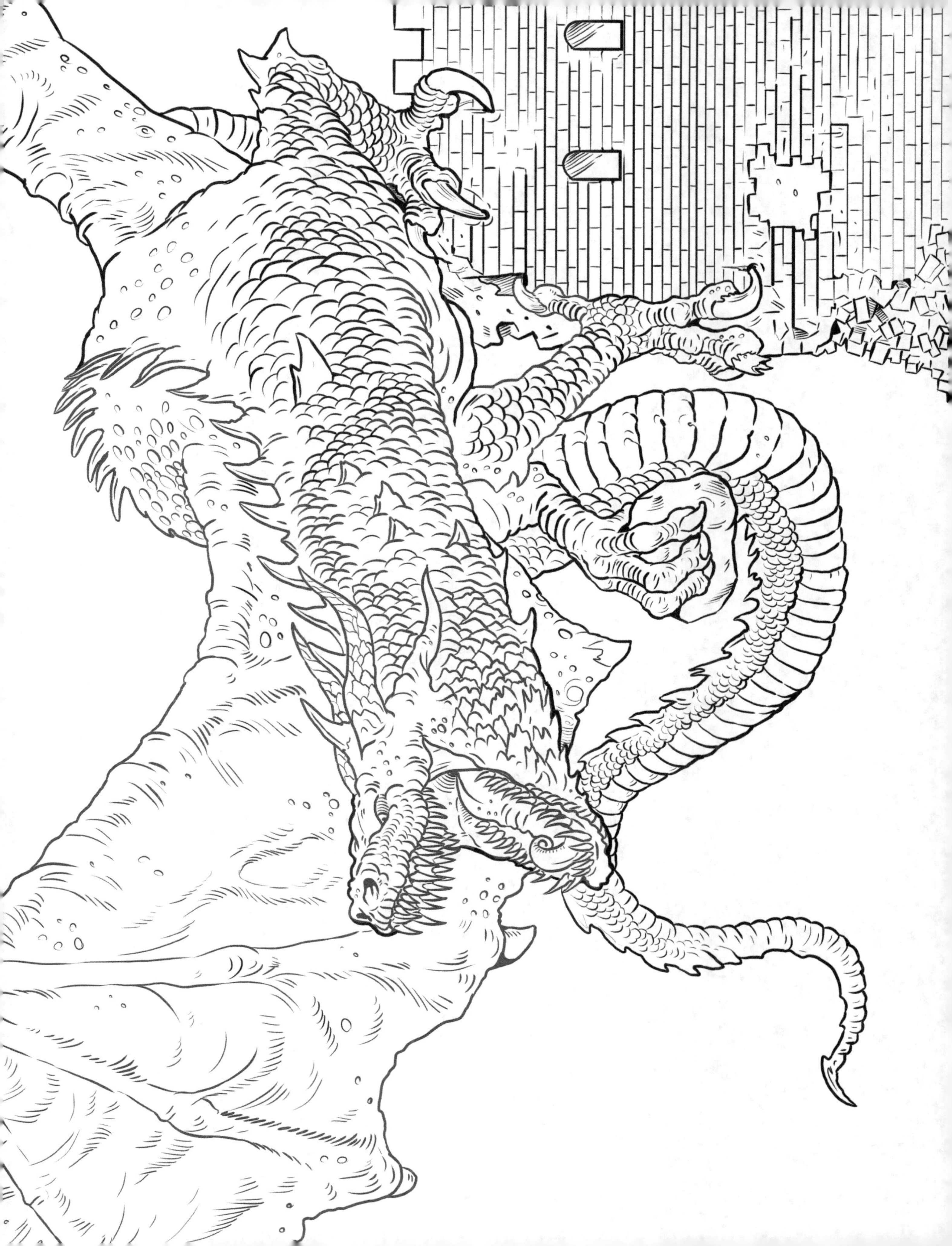

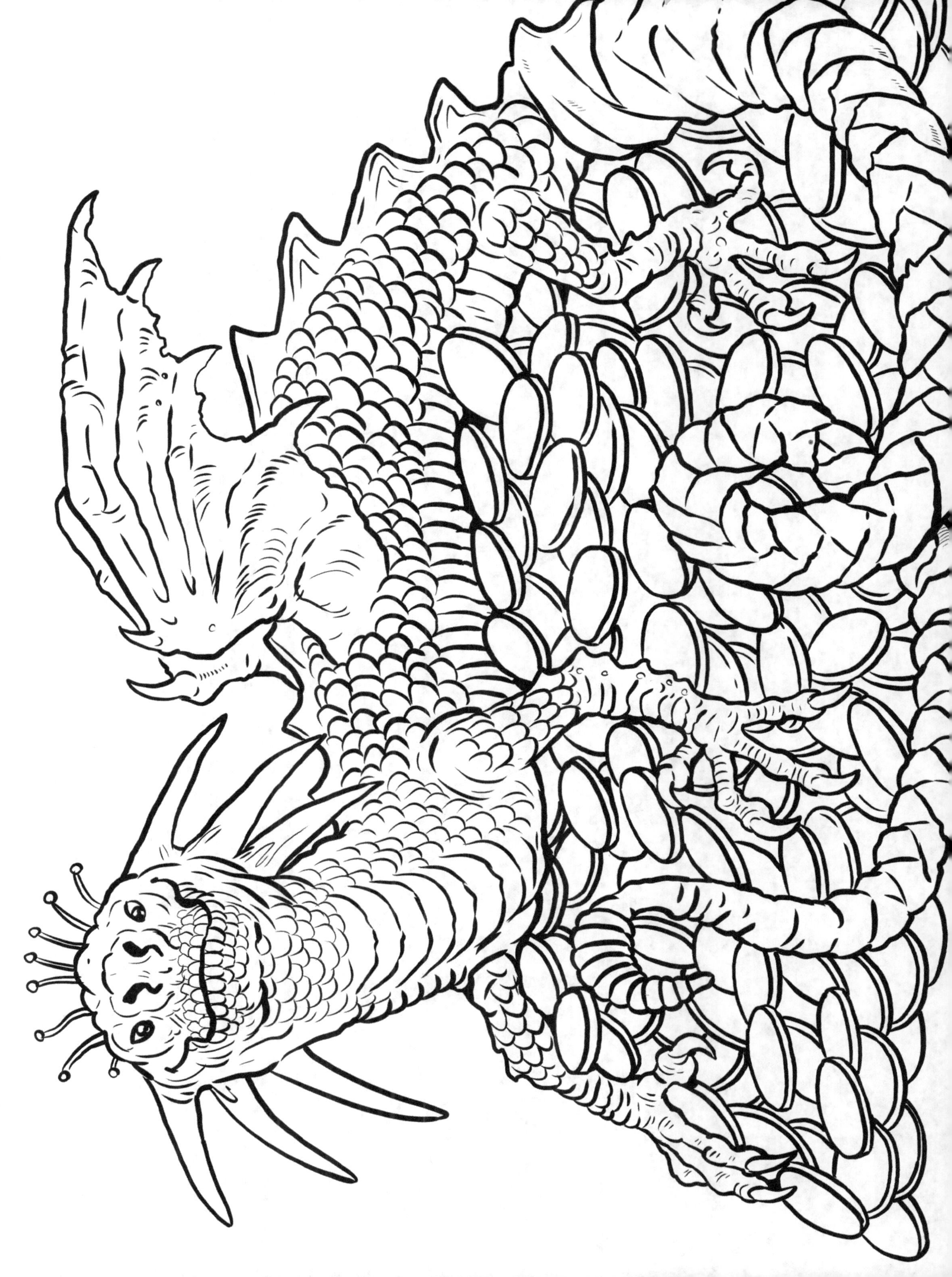

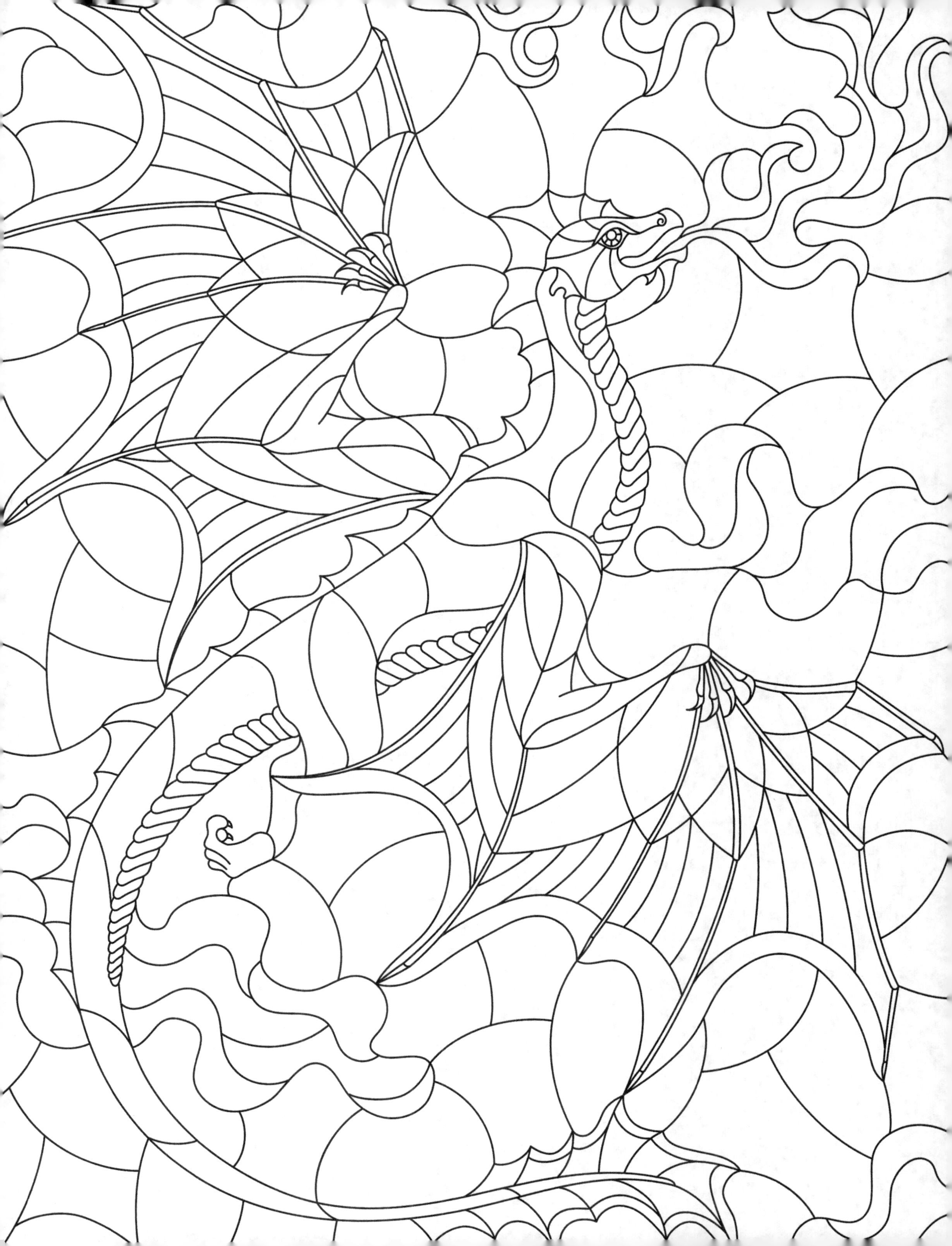

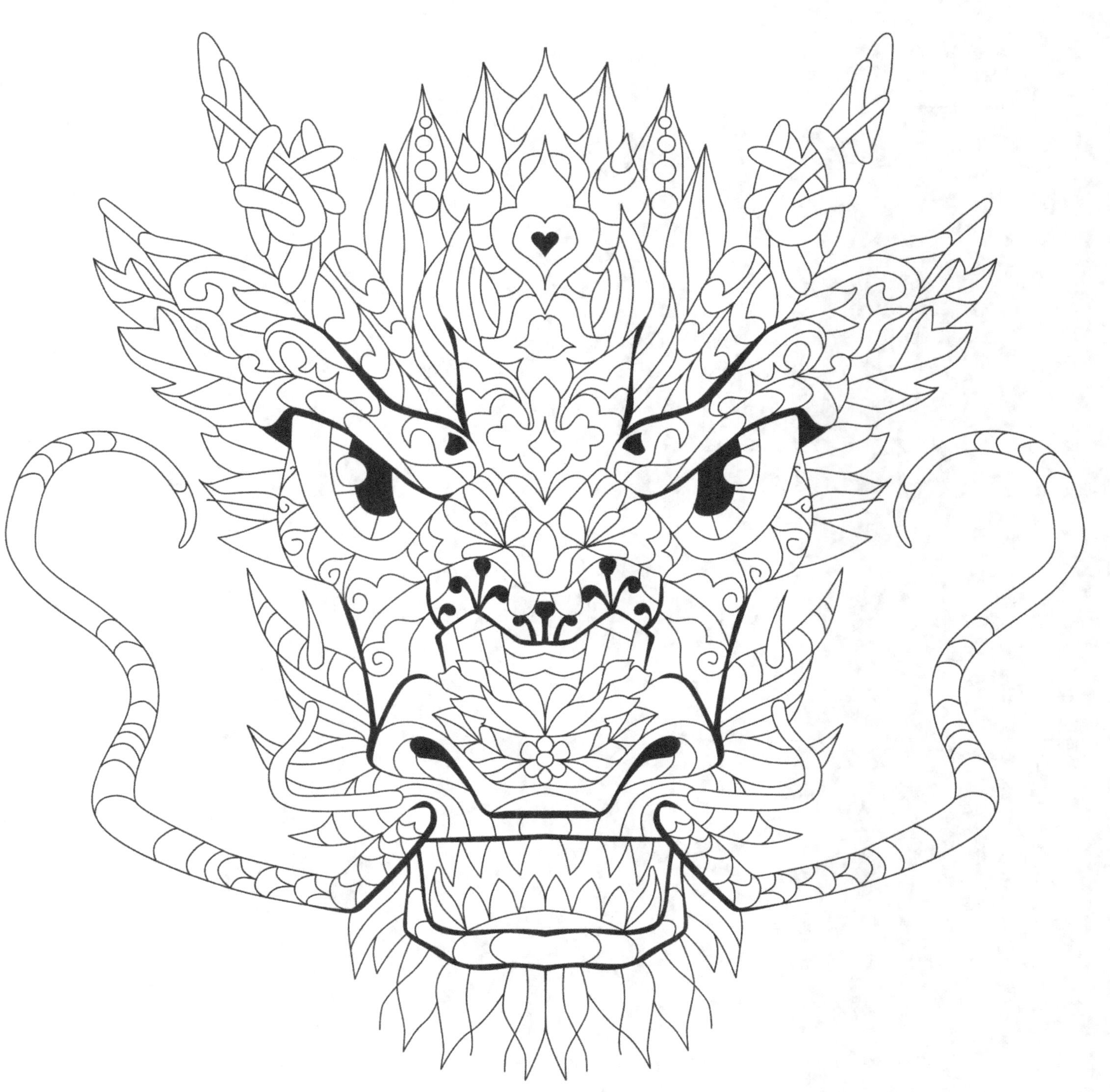